The Church of Christ

Pursuing God's Goals for His Church in a Divided Religious World

Tim Alsup

Cross-Shaped Publishing

Arlington, TN

The Church of Christ

Cross-Shaped Publishing
6131 Chester Street
Arlington, TN 38002

Cover Design by Melissa Ellis Smith

Book Layout ©2017 BookDesignTemplates.com

Cross Icon from www.freepik.com. Used on condition of attribution as stated on the site, October 2017

The Church of Christ/ Tim Alsup. —1st ed.

ISBN-13: 978-0692053058 (Cross-Shaped Publishing)

ISBN-10: 0692053050

Table of Contents

Thank you to Arinne, for your constant love and encouragement in life, faith, and ministry.

Thank you to Mom and Dad, for your faithful parenting that made sure Christ and His church were always present in our lives.

Thank you to the Great Oaks youth group – you were the first to go through this study as a Bible class on our Fall 2016 Wednesday nights, and your good questions and thoughts helped make this book better.

Thank you to the Great Oaks church family: you have been a blessing to our family and our faith, and we love your example of genuinely trying to be everything God wants His people to be.

Husbands, love your wives, just as Christ also loved the church
and gave Himself up for her,

so that He might sanctify her, having cleansed her
by the washing of water with the word,

that He might present to Himself the church in all her glory,
having no spot or wrinkle or any such thing;
but that she would be holy and blameless.

— Ephesians 5:25-27

Introduction: The Goals of This Book...

What do we believe and practice in churches of Christ?

We first wanted a book to share with people who are interested in knowing more about churches of Christ. Like other churches, our church assemblies have visitors from a variety of religious backgrounds – many with no religious background – who naturally have questions about what we believe in churches of Christ. We wanted to do better than just a brief conversation in the lobby. And in everyday life, we find that faith discussions come up randomly, in driveways and waiting rooms and break rooms, times when you least expect them, and in circumstances that don't always allow the full study such topics deserve. So we wanted to be able to hand visitors or friends a book that explained some of our goals, giving them the opportunity to learn more about our desire to simply be undenominational followers of Jesus Christ, and letting them privately think through what the Bible teaches about God's goals for His church.

I also wanted to write this book for those of us who are already part of churches of Christ. My experience in churches of Christ is that from teenagers up through our older generations, there is always a great deal of interest in what we believe and why. We realize that our religious world has lots of different ideas, and so we think it's important to regularly reflect on our own goals and understandings, either to understand them for the first time, or to reaffirm them and deepen them, trying to make sure we are on a path that is pleasing to God. We also have great interest in these types of topics because of how often we hear people – many even from within churches of Christ – who either misunderstand or misrepresent our goals, producing confusion or discouragement or worse, and obscuring what most of us believe is a valuable message that our world needs to hear.

So I wanted to put this study together to explore some of the "who we're trying to be" issues. I am hopeful it will be a good resource, appropriate for visitors, friends, Bible classes, or personal reading, and meaningful for teens, college-aged, young adults, or adults. While writing it, here are some of the goals I tried to keep in mind:

Content - I wanted to explore some of the major belief-and-practice decisions that all churches must make, looking at what the Bible says about them, and explaining the ways churches of Christ are trying to honor God's word in our beliefs and practices.

Understandable - I wanted to present those ideas in a way that was clear and understandable to anyone, no matter their religious background.

Tone - I wanted to discuss everything in a way that was Christ-centered, Bible-teaching, and God-honoring. I wanted to make sure the "issues" were addressed in a way that showed kindness to everyone, consistent with the "truth in love" goal of Ephesians 4:15.

Relevant - I wanted to make sure we considered questions that people are asking in today's culture, including relevant questions about each issue, but also addressing modern-day foundational questions such as whether the church should matter in our faith at all, and how modern-day religious ideas affect the way churches define their goals.

Multi-purpose - I have included discussion and reflection questions in each chapter, and I anticipate they will be helpful when using the book for Bible classes or small group studies. I also hope the questions will be meaningful in personal study, allowing the reader a space for processing the chapter and reflecting on how it might affect our lives personally.

Perspective - I wanted the book to keep these various topics connected and in perspective with one another. Many of these topics could easily be a much longer study on their own, but I wanted to put them in a book that covered them all under one roof, in a relatively succinct way. By lining them up together so closely, my hope is that we will see the connections between them, specifically how they all connect back to Christ and to the big-picture goals that God gave His church.

You, of course, can decide for yourself whether this book accomplishes any of those goals, but those are some of the things I was aiming for in putting this study together. I hope it's a blessing to you in one way or another.

Living in a divided religious world, we need to make time to reflect on who God wants us to be, and to reflect together in the right tone and the right spirit. I look forward to studying along with you over the next 13 chapters, and I pray it will help us all recommit ourselves to understanding and making the church what God wants it to be…

In Christ,

Tim

Section 1:
Does the Church Matter?

CHAPTER 1

Why Are There So Many Churches?

"I also say to you that you are Peter, and upon this rock I will build My church; and the gates of Hades will not overpower it."
-Jesus, in Matthew 16:18

Starters

- How many different religious groups can you name that are trying to follow Jesus, but are divided into different names and denominations?
- Why do you think there are so many denominations? Do you think God wants it that way?
- How do you think different people would answer this question: "Does Church Matter?"
- If you are part of churches of Christ, how would you describe the churches of Christ to a friend? If you are not part of churches of Christ, what do you know about them?

Looking For Answers

Like everyone else raised in a church in our divided religious culture, I eventually began asking questions. Why do we pass 12 church buildings – all with different denominational names – before we get to the one where we worship? How is our church different from my friend's church? Why are we separated by different names and beliefs, when we are all supposed to be following Jesus? Surely this wasn't the way God wanted it.

Soon, my fellow teenagers in the youth group began sharing similar questions. Sometimes it was sitting around after an afternoon of basketball, when post-game conversation on the porch steps occasionally turned into more-serious questions about faith and life. Sometimes it was out by the car after an evening youth devotional. Sometimes it was in the back seat of the van on the way to a youth retreat. It became obvious that we all wanted to know why things were so fractured in our religious world – and what we should do about it.

Our questions eventually got back to our preacher, who had two teenage children with us in the youth group. To our surprise and appreciation, he made us an offer: he would teach a Bible class for us teenagers, with the promise that we could ask any question we wanted. He would discuss some of the differences in the religious world, and why our church family believed and practiced what we did. What's more, he promised us that our discussions would simply follow wherever the Bible led, and that he would be open to whatever Scripture taught, just as he hoped we would be. He assured us that he wouldn't just give us his opinions or canned answers, but instead we would look up the answers to each question in the Bible, where he would let us read what the Bible says, and we could then decide for ourselves.

Looking back, I realize I was blessed with many good Bible classes through the years, but that particular class is still one that stands out. In fact, I still feel the impact that class had on my faith. I don't remember all the topics we discussed, but what I remember about that class was the *spirit*. We were simply going to search the Bible. We were going to find what God wanted. And then we would do it God's way.

Doing It God's Way

Trying to do things God's way is what this book is all about. The spirit of that teenage Bible class highlighted the types of things I often heard growing up in churches of Christ. "We simply want to be undenominational Christians." "We simply want to follow the Bible." "We don't want to get caught up following man's traditions over God's traditions."

After I went away to college, I went through another time of questioning religious division, and of comparing different beliefs. Was I attending a "church of Christ" just because I had always gone to one, or was what they taught truly what God wanted? Through several life rounds of asking questions and exploring religious teachings, I kept coming back to the importance of those goals I heard growing up: let's simply be Christians, let's simply follow the Bible. I have traveled down the path far enough to learn that those things can't always be done "simply," but I've only become more convinced that they are the right goals. Whatever the shortcomings among those of us in churches of Christ (and since we are people who fall short like everyone else, I'm sure we each have plenty of shortcomings), I believe the goals of undenominational, Bible-based Christianity are the right goals, because they are the ones God gave His church. The harder-to-answer questions often come before we study God's goals for His church, questions like: "do I care enough to search for what God wants?" Or "do I have the spiritual courage to follow what God wants if it's different from what I've always heard, or different from what I want?"

Which brings us back to our broken religious world. The prevailing attitude seems to be that people don't care. People criticize the idea of church far more than they encourage it. I know many people who have simply given up on church, for various reasons. You know many of them also. Some people say church just isn't that important as long as you have faith. Jesus is what matters, not the church, they say. Is that what God thinks?

And among those who haven't given up on the idea of church, most of them seem comfortable in their fenced-off corner of denominationalism. We tell each other that our differences don't really matter, or that God doesn't care. We say that as long as you "go to church" you are doing great. I dislike confrontation and ruffled feelings as much as the next person, but it has always left me asking: Is that true? Or is that just what we wish to be true, so that we don't really have to face the difficult questions? Have we ever slowed down long enough to dig in to what God says about it?

So those two big problems – giving up on the idea of church altogether, or deciding that "where I go to church" doesn't matter – are the ones we will consider first, and they will be the focus of the next two chapters. But before we get there, we can go ahead and start giving partial answers to those problems, by going back to Jesus...

It All Starts With Jesus...

So does church matter? It helps to remember where the church came from. It wasn't just that someone decided, "Hey, we should get a group of people together and call it a church." The plan for church had much deeper roots than an idea of men. In fact, Ephesians 1:4 says that God planned to call men together in Christ "before the foundation of the world."

And that's how this idea of church began. God planned to send His Son, Jesus Christ, to bring people back to God in spite of their sins. Jesus would bring teachings that would transform lives. He would die on the cross for the sins of all mankind. And He would also establish a new people – a people based not in race or language or color or nationality, but a people united spiritually with God and each other through Jesus Christ. He would call it the church.

Remember the conversation Jesus had with His disciples in Matthew 16:13-18? He called them away to a region called Caesarea Philippi, and while there, He asked them, "Who do people say that the Son of Man is?" After they gave several responses, Jesus then asked them pointedly, "But who do you say that I am?" Peter spoke up, declaring that Jesus is "the Christ, the Son of the living God." Jesus said that Peter was absolutely right, and that Jesus would build something on the foundation of that truth:

"I also say to you that you are Peter,
and upon this rock I will build My church;
and the gates of Hades will not overpower it."
-Jesus, in Matthew 16:18

So who "built" the church? Jesus Himself! And whose church would it be? Jesus called it "My" church. Church is Jesus' idea, and the church belongs to Him.

And in case we have any questions about how much Jesus loves the church, look at how Paul described the church when talking to some church elders in Acts 20:

> *"Be on guard for yourselves and for all the flock,*
> *among which the Holy Spirit has made you overseers,*
> *to shepherd <u>the church of God which He purchased</u>*
> *<u>with His own blood</u>."*
> *-Paul to the Ephesian elders, in Acts 20:28*

Jesus loved the church so much that He "purchased it," not with money but with His own blood. How many things do you love so much that you would be willing to die for them? For most of us, not very many. But Jesus loved the church so much that He died for it.

So does the church matter in our faith? We must remember: the church wasn't something that people invented, this came from Jesus Christ Himself!

What Jesus Wants His Church to Be

So what about all the division in our religious world? Is that what Jesus wanted His church to be? Well, you might notice in Matthew 16:18 that Jesus built a "church" (singular), not "churches" (plural), pointing to the unity He wanted His people to have. There would be local churches in many places – the New Testament tells us of churches in Jerusalem and in Corinth and in Rome and so on. Paul refers to the "churches of Christ" in Romans 16:16 to describe these local churches. But these local churches were all to be united through Christ, as the one "church" Jesus built. We weren't supposed to be divided into different denominational groups; we were all supposed to be united in *one* church.

On the night before Jesus was crucified, He made this even more clear as He prayed to the Father:

> *"I do not ask on behalf of these alone, but for those also who believe in Me through their word; <u>that they may all be one</u>; even as You, Father, are in Me and I in You, that they also may be in Us, so that the world may believe that You sent Me. The glory which You have given Me I have given to them, <u>that they may be one, just as We are one</u>; I in them and You in Me, <u>that they may be perfected in unity</u>, so that the world may know that You sent Me, and love them, even as You have loved Me."*
> *-Jesus' prayer, in John 17:20-23*

We notice several things in that passage. First, Jesus is praying for those who would believe through the apostles' words, which includes us! Jesus prayed for you and me and for all who follow Him, which is encouraging to think about. Second, He prayed that believers would have the same unity with each other that Jesus has with the Father. That's a high standard of unity! The Father and Son (and Spirit) are all united in perfect harmony and purpose, and that's what Jesus wanted His church to have. Third, He said the church's unity could show the world that Jesus was truly from God. The world should be able to see the unity of the church – people from all backgrounds bound together in Christ – and grow in love for the church and for God.

Wow, our religious world has really messed that up, hasn't it? When the world sees people who are trying to follow Jesus, they don't see unity. They see division and disharmony. Jesus had a different vision for His followers: He wanted them to be united together, imitating the unity of the Godhead (Father, Son, Spirit).

And if Jesus' prayer in John 17 wasn't clear enough, look at what Paul told the Corinthian church later about dividing into human names:

"Now I exhort you, brethren, by the name of our Lord Jesus Christ, that you all agree and that there be no divisions among you, but that you be made complete in the same mind and in the same judgment. For I have been informed concerning you, my brethren, by Chloe's people, that there are quarrels among you. Now I mean this, that each one of you is saying, "I am of Paul," and "I of Apollos," and "I of Cephas," and "I of Christ." Has Christ been divided? Paul was not crucified for you, was he? Or were you baptized in the name of Paul?"
-Paul to the Corinthian Church, in 1 Corinthians 1:10-13

That passage calls most of our religious world to repent, doesn't it? Paul says there should be no divisions among those who follow Jesus. And he says we should not take any other name besides the name of Christ! There should be no Paul-Christians or Apollos-Christians or Cephas-Christians. Today, it means there should be no Baptist-Christians or Catholic-Christians or Methodist-Christians, and that list could go for a long time, couldn't it? We are not saying anything unkind about the motives of those in denominational groups, but Scripture is clear: God doesn't want us to take human names, He wants us only to take the name of Christ. Our divided-into-manmade-names religious world is not want God wanted His church to be.

So Jesus intended His church to be one. United and undivided. Taking only the name of Christ. We've really messed that up through the years. But that doesn't mean God has stopped wanting us to get it right. God still wants us to try to be undenominational Christians, just as He taught.

The Church of Christ

So what is the church of Christ? It's the one church Jesus established, the one we read about in the Bible. Those of us today who claim only the "church of Christ" are not claiming a denominational identity. We take "church of Christ" not as a denominational name, but as a biblical description of the undenominational church Christ built. Our goal is to simply be part of that one church Jesus died for. Not part of a fenced-off corner of denominationalism with a human name on the sign. As we've just seen, God doesn't want that. God wants us to be followers of Jesus. Christians. Nothing more and nothing less. We are trying to tear down denominational fences and man-made names, and stand simply as Christians in Christ's church.

And we encourage everyone who wants to follow Jesus to do the same thing: to see God's plan for His church and follow it. Don't just fall in line with a religious world that has accepted denominationalism. Instead, pursue what Jesus wanted: undenominational, New Testament Christianity. We hope you will join us in that goal!

Where We're Going...

So I am hopeful this book will help us dig in to what God wants in His church. I realize it's a controversial subject, because there are so many different opinions and ideas and traditions, but I hope we will find the desire and the courage to search for God's way. We will not say anything unkind about anyone's heart or sincerity – I try to assume people are sincere until they prove otherwise. This book will not be unkind toward any religious group or try to make anyone look bad; I've got friends and family in other religious groups just like you do. We will simply try to compare modern day practices to God's ideals for His church as they are found in Scripture, and challenge all of us to follow God's plan.

Here's where we are going:

- In Chapters 2 and 3, we will continue exploring the question, "Does the Church Matter?" Those discussions will build on what we just saw about the church being God's plan, not ours.
- Chapters 4-8 will explore a powerful biblical concept sometimes called "restoration," in a section entitled "Getting Back to God's Plan for His Church."
- Chapters 9-10 will help us complete the big picture of God's goals for His church, reminding us of two essential goals that churches sometimes struggle with, in a section titled "Remembering the Big Picture: Two Other Essential Pieces of God's Plan."
- Chapters 11-12 will examine some of the challenges we face in pursuing undenominational Christianity amidst a divided religious world. Those chapters are entitled "Keeping Perspective in a Divided Religious World."
- And Chapter 13 will give us one final look at "Becoming The Church God Wants Us To Be."

I can promise you the same thing our preacher promised us years ago: I simply want to find what God wants and do it His way. So if you see something in this book that's not biblical, please let me know. I've done my best to accurately share what we find in Scripture, but if I've missed the mark, please tell me; and please be patient with me, as I promise to keep searching and digging myself.

I've come to believe that God is much more serious about His church than we are often led to believe. And I'm naïve enough to believe that God's goals for His church are still possible, if we will only care enough to pursue them.

But just as I was told years ago, I'll let you see what the Bible says, and you can decide for yourself...

Discussion Questions

1) Have you had a time in your life when you were comparing religious beliefs and trying to discover what was right? What caused you to start asking questions? Did you reach any temporary conclusions? What questions do you still have?
2) If you have ever been in Bible studies that discussed religious beliefs, did it feel like it was more to 'defend the church creed' or more like 'let's just see what the Bible says?' Why? Which approach seems more reasonable to you and why?
3) What passages lead us to believe that the church is really important to God?
4) What are some of the main goals of those who take the descriptive name "churches of Christ?" Do those goals sound like the right goals to you? Why or why not? How are they different from others in the religious world?
5) Is denominationalism right in God's eyes? What passages tell us what God thinks about religious division? Why do you think people have accepted denominationalism and man-made names?

6) Do you think people want to be more united in Christ? Why or why not?
7) Can it be difficult to discuss religious differences in a Christ-like spirit? Why? Read Galatians 5:22-23 and think about how the "fruit of the Spirit" should be applied in discussing religious differences.

Personal Reflection

1) Please stop and pray that God will bless us as we begin this study together. Pray that we will bring the right attitude—one of sincere humility and truth-seeking. Pray that we will find and understand the truth. Pray that our religious world will see where we've all messed up God's plan and pray that we will all have the help of God to make it better.
2) What has your attitude been toward the church? We have seen in this chapter that Jesus has a high view of the church – loving it enough to die for it. Have you shared Jesus' high view of the church?
3) What are you doing to build unity in Christ's church, the type of unity Christ prayed for? Have your words and actions been bringing greater unity or greater division to your own church family? How can you do better?

CHAPTER 2

Does Church Matter?

(Is It Possible To Have Jesus Without The Church?)

"Christ also loved the church and gave Himself up for her,... that He might present to Himself the church in all her glory..."
-Paul, in Ephesians 5:25-27

Starters

- Do you know anybody who has given up on the idea of church? Why?
- If you could talk to someone who is giving up on church, how would you encourage them to give church another chance?
- Can you be fulfilling God's ideal plan for your life without the church? Why or why not?

I'm Never Going Back

Our divided religious culture includes a lot of bitterness toward "church," leading some people to reject the idea of church altogether. I was knocking doors and inviting people to church one afternoon in the small town of Eddyville, Kentucky, when a sweet elderly woman answered the door. At least, she seemed sweet when I introduced myself, until I handed her a flyer and told her we'd love to have her visit with the church for worship services sometime. I hoped it sounded as sincere as I meant it. She had started to reach for the flyer, but as she heard me say "church," she pulled her hand back and became visibly upset. She looked up at me angrily, and said in a stern voice, "You don't have anything in that church building that I don't have right here in my house!" And before I could even absorb the words, the door was shut. That had rarely happened in door knocking – most people were very kind and many were very appreciative – so I stood on the porch step for a second in shock. What had just happened?

I walked away wondering what could have happened in that woman's life for her to feel so angry toward the idea of church. Had she ever been to church? Did she just not like Christians for some reason? Or, since she said she had all she needed in her own house, did she consider herself a Christian, but for some reason hated church? If I hadn't been a little scared of her, I might have gone back to ask!

As years have gone on, I've met others who didn't like the idea of church, and some seemed just as bitter as that woman did. You have probably met them too. Perhaps some of your personal friends have gone down that path. For that matter, you may have lived through similar stories of your own. Those stories often go something like this:

"One lady at church said something critical and rude to me, and others were talking about me behind my back...I will never go back to a church again."

Or...

"I knew too many of those guys, and I knew some of them were complete hypocrites. If that's what Christians are, I don't want anything to do with it. You won't see me in a church ever again."

Or...

"I used to go to church. I watched a church split over the smallest issues; people just couldn't get along. It was the biggest mess you've ever seen; people yelling, gossiping, lying. I promised myself I would never set foot in a church again."

You've heard stories like this, haven't you? They come from people who used to attend church, had a bad experience, and decided it wasn't for them.

There are at least 2 reasons stories like this feel somewhat common:

1) *First, the church is made up of people.* People will eventually fail us, because we are all sinful. So if you are around a church long enough, you will see people do things that are against the spirit and ideals of Christianity. They will disappoint you, and you might be tempted to give up on church altogether, even though their actions don't accurately represent what "church" should be striving for.

2) *Second, we hear these stories so often because about 1 in 3 Americans today are "de-churched."*[1] For every 3 people you pass in the grocery store, 1 of them used to be actively involved in some sort of church before they decided to just stop going. Something happened, and they quit church. If that survey is right, there are well over 100 million "de-churched" people in America. No wonder we all know people who have these types of "why I quit the church" stories.

Jesus Without the Church?

People decide that church doesn't matter for different reasons. Some have had bad experiences and became bitter, but that's only one reason of many. Some are selfish with their time and decide not to be part of church. Some want to live sinful lifestyles and therefore they try to avoid places where godly lifestyles are taught and encouraged. Some people simply don't believe in Jesus, and so of course they don't think church is important.

But the strangest category of people who say church doesn't matter are those who consider themselves followers of Jesus, yet have nothing to do with church. I say this is a "strange" category because they apparently misunderstand the plan of Jesus for our lives. Remember what we saw in the last chapter: Jesus built the church (Matthew 16:18) and He loved it enough to die for it (Acts 20:28). The church is the plan of Jesus and it is made up of those who have received salvation through His death. So whether we like it or not, having a right relationship with God through Jesus puts

---

[1] George Barna and David Kinnaman, *Churchless*, ebook published by Tyndale, September 19, 2014. Their results summarized in a chart on the website: https://www.barna.com/churchless/ accessed November 30, 2017.

us into fellowship with the church – with others who are also right with God through Jesus (1 John 1:3). The church automatically becomes our family through Jesus Christ.

Now if you don't believe in Jesus as God's Son, I understand why you don't think church matters. I would, however, encourage you to study what Christians believe about Jesus. I think you will find that there are compelling reasons to believe that Jesus is exactly who He said He is – God's Son who came to earth – and that His sacrifice for our sins is the greatest act of love the world has ever seen. The more you study it and reflect on it, the more I think you will grow in faith and love for Christ.

But if you already try to follow Christ, with a faith in Christ and a love for Christ, then you should be aware that the church is part of the plan. Jesus simply doesn't come without the church! As Acts 2:47 put it: "And the Lord was adding to their number day by day those who were being saved." When you are saved, God adds you to "their number," to those who are in His church. You can request a hamburger without ketchup; you can order a drink with no ice; but you can't have Christ without His church – Jesus just doesn't come that way! When we realize that close biblical connection between Christ and His church, it will re-shape the way we view the church.

A Different View of the Church

If any Christian would have had a reason to hate the church, it was Paul. He was as sincere as they came. Jesus had appeared to him personally (the story, which happened when he was known as "Saul," is in Acts chapter 9 if you've never read it before), and so he believed in Jesus with all his heart. Paul felt he had a new mission in life: a mission of living for

Christ. But after He became a Christian, look at what happened:

"When he came to Jerusalem, he was trying to associate with the disciples; but they were all afraid of him, not believing that he was a disciple." -Acts 9:26

The Christians in the church at Jerusalem wouldn't even talk to Paul when he first came! We may understand why – after all, he had been active in having Christians killed before he became a Christian himself – but it must have been discouraging and humiliating for Paul, who was trying to turn his life around.

Later in his life, in a church Paul had helped start in the city of Corinth, there were people criticizing him and making fun of him behind his back. Look at what Paul said about his critics in 2 Corinthians 10:10:

"For they say, 'His letters are weighty and strong, but his personal presence is unimpressive and his speech contemptible.'"

So Paul could've told his own negative stories about church:

He could've said: *"When I went to church in Jerusalem, no one would even talk to me. They all whispered behind my back that they didn't believe I was a real Christian. All they could talk about was my past."* (See Acts 9:26)

Or he could've said: *"I helped start the church in Corinth. Now all they do is criticize me when I'm not around. I'm just trying to follow Jesus and help others, but they keep badmouthing me. They say I'm weak. They criticize my speaking ability. They say I'm not trustworthy, and that I'm not even a real apostle."* (See 2 Cor. 10:1,10)

If Paul were like most people, he would've followed those stories by saying: "so I will never go back to church again."

But instead of hating the church, do you know who absolutely loved the church? Paul. The same guy who had experienced some mistreatment from Christians who were not living up to Christian standards. He poured his life into encouraging churches and planting new churches all over the Roman world. How could Paul love the church so much? What did he understand that we often miss?

The Secret People Often Miss

I think you see the secret in the Book of Ephesians, which was written by Paul. In Ephesians, you find Paul speaking about the church in majestic terms. It's much different from what we often hear today. Inspired by the Spirit of God, Paul wrote that the church is:

- **The body of Christ (Eph. 1:22-23).** What does that mean? When Christ's physical body was on earth, He spent His life helping, teaching, and encouraging faith in others. Now that Christ has ascended back to the Father, the church is His earthly body. The church is the group that does what Jesus did: helping, teaching, encouraging. Yes, Christians sometimes don't live up to their God-given goals, but on the other hand, can we even count the good done by Christians acting in the world as the body of Christ?
- **The household of Christ (Eph. 2:19-22).** Family is special. And when family doesn't feel special to us, we wish it did, because we see the value of a family that stands with us and loves us. The church is Christ's household: His family, the people who share a deeper closeness

with each other and with Him. Verse 22 adds that this household is where God lives!

- **The voice of Christ (Eph. 3:10).** The church is God's voice in the world to proclaim His wisdom. God has told us the truth about the world: creation, sin, salvation, eternity. But we won't hear that story from news organizations or movies or the world's voices. Who will tell people the truth about life and about the things that really matter? The church, standing as the voice for God in the world, holding up His message for all who will listen.
- **The bride of Christ (Eph. 5:25-27,32).** I know my wife isn't perfect, but if I heard you criticizing her constantly or talking rudely about her, I would be upset. I love her; how dare you speak badly of her! The church is the bride of Christ, the bride Jesus loved enough to die for. I wonder how Jesus feels when we overly-criticize His church or act like it's not important. Jesus "loves" the church – it's His bride!

In those descriptions we find the secret to Paul's love for the church, and it's a secret that many people are missing. What is it?

In each of those passages, Paul connects his high view of the church to his high view of Jesus Christ. He doesn't say he loves the church because the people are always perfect and the preacher is always excellent and the worship is always a great experience. It's not human perfection that made the church special to Paul.

What made the church special? Paul realized the close connection between Christ and His church. Paul loved the church because he loved Jesus Christ. And since Jesus Christ loved the church and lived in the church, Paul wasn't going to quit on it, in spite of the imperfect – and sometimes downright mean – people he found there. He would pour out his life to make it stronger and better, out of a love for the Savior who built it and bought it.

If You Love Me...

It reminds me of what Jesus said to Peter. In John 21:15-17, the resurrected Jesus is getting Peter back to the mission of being an apostle. Jesus asks 3 times if Peter loves Him. All 3 times Peter says yes. And all 3 times Jesus replies: then feed My sheep. Who are His sheep? His people. His church.

Notice the train of thought: Peter, if you love Me, then join My mission to help My church.

"But Jesus, they were hypocrites!" we might say. Jesus might reply: "Yes, but you've been a hypocrite at times also, and I still love you. If you love Me, feed My sheep."

"But Jesus, didn't you hear what they said to me?!" "Yes, but I've heard you say some pretty mean things too, and I still love you. If you love Me, feed My sheep."

The Church of Christ

Does the church matter? It matters to Jesus – He built it and bought it! So if we truly love Jesus, we will look at the church differently than most people do. Loving the church because of the people will only go so far. Loving the church because you like how they act will only go so far. We must go deeper than that, to Christ Himself.

If we love Jesus, like Paul and Peter did, we will feed His sheep. We will join Jesus in pouring out our lives to help make His church a little more like the majestic bride He wants it to be. He wants to present the church "in all her glory" (Eph. 5:27) at the end of time. And He wants you and I to be part of that plan. When we become a Christian, He adds us to His people – His family – and that's where He wants us to serve and grow.

Christ's church needs you. It needs you not to give up on its failures. It needs you to show others what it means to love Jesus. It needs you to help it serve and show Christ's body and voice to the world. Paul believed in that mission, because his Savior believed in that mission.

Do you love Jesus? If so, don't ignore what He calls us to do: let's keep loving and building up His church.

What's Next...

There's another side to the idea that church doesn't matter: many people say it doesn't matter which church you are part of, "as long as you go to church." Is that what the Bible teaches? That's a loaded question – and it could be something that all of us need to think about! In the next chapter, we will see what we can find in Scripture about whether it matters which church we are identified with. And if we find it does matter, we'll consider what should we do about it...

Discussion Questions

1) Do you know someone who loves the church? How can you tell? Why do you think they love the church so much?
2) Why might someone want to "have Jesus but not the church?"
3) If you were Paul, how would you have reacted to the way he was treated in Jerusalem or Corinth? Do you

understand why people in Jerusalem were afraid of him? What do you admire about Paul's response?

4) When people in the church fail us or act in un-Christian ways (and they will), how should we respond? How should the church respond? Read 2 Timothy 2:24-26, Matthew 18:15-18, and Galatians 6:1 as part of your discussion.

5) God knew that Christians in the church would sometimes fail each other, yet He still established the church. Why do you think He felt it was so important to bring us into closer fellowship with each other? What are some of the blessings of a church family that stand out to you?

6) We saw that Ephesians 2:19 refers to the church as a family. Read Mark 3:20-21,31-35. What does this passage tell us about Jesus' perspective on physical family and spiritual family? What does it say about the relationship between Jesus and His followers?

7) Why do you think God called the church the "bride" of Christ in Ephesians 5:25-33? What might that teach us about the church's relationship to Christ?

Personal Reflection

1) If Jesus came to you and asked you if you loved Him (like He did to Peter in John 21), how would you answer? How do you think He would respond? Would He say anything about your relationship to His people, like He did to Peter?

2) How have I acted toward Christians who have wronged me or wronged God in how they acted? Have I given up on them too quickly?

3) Think of a time when you failed, but someone still showed you grace and patience. What did that mean to you? Should you pass that same grace and patience along to others, including others in the church? Why is it sometimes difficult to show grace and patience to others, especially in the church?

CHAPTER 3

Does "Where I Go To Church" Matter?

(Does God Really Care, As Long As I Just Go To Church Somewhere?)

"But in the following instructions I do not commend you,
because when you come together it is
not for the better but for the worse."
-Paul, in 1 Corinthians 11:17

Starters

- Have you ever had to choose for yourself which church you would be a part of? How did you choose? How do you think most people choose their church home?
- Is it possible for someone to call themselves a Christian, but not actually be pleasing to God? If so, how?

- Is it possible for a group of people to call themselves a church, but not actually be pleasing to God? If so, how?
- What determines if a church is a "good church?"

How Should I Choose a Church?

David was moving to a new town. He had graduated from college and accepted a job as a teacher. It was his first job, and it was also his first time to move to a new place by himself. Sure, he had gone to college, but there he had lived in the dorms and basically did what everyone else at college did. This was different. He was moving to a place where he knew almost nobody, and he had lots of decisions to make before his school year started. Where would he live? What type of house should he live in? What would he do about insurance? How would he budget and spend his paychecks? So many decisions that he had never had to consider before now.

In the midst of his many "new town" decisions, David realized he needed to make another important decision that he had never made by himself: what would he do about church? He had grown up going to church with his family, and had become a Christian as a teenager. In college, he would go to various local congregations – not quite as often as he knew he should have – and he had often gone back home on weekends, where he would simply go to worship with his family just like he had growing up.

But now, he was in a new town by himself, and he suddenly felt the importance of making his own decision about faith and church. He thought through the temptation not to go to church at all. Those not-so-good thoughts tried to tell him that he didn't have to follow his parents' rules anymore, and that maybe he should show his "independence" by living a life without church. But that option only caused him to reflect deeper on what he believed personally, and he realized that he truly believed in God, in Christ, and in Christ's church, just as he had learned from the Bible while growing up. Yes, he would go to church. He knew that was the right thing. But where would he go?

David remembered passing a few church buildings in town, so he pulled out his laptop and began an internet search to learn more about them. Soon he found himself searching through a long list of churches in the area, a list that included all sorts of different names and denominations. The search results themselves brought up a question that he instantly realized needed some more thought: how should I choose a church?

The Church of Your Preference?

Have you ever had to make that decision for yourself? I have sometimes wondered what someone with no religious background would do if they suddenly decided they wanted to start going to church. With all the different church names and options, where would you even start?

If you asked around about how to make a decision about church, my guess is that most people would say something like, "It doesn't really matter where you go to church, as long as you go." They would then tell you that since it doesn't matter where you go, you can pick your church based on your own personal preferences. Just decide which preacher you like best, or which worship style you prefer, or what service times fit your schedule, or which church seems most popular in the community, or just go wherever you happen to make friends first.

But if you and I are deciding where to go to church for ourselves, I hope we will slow down before we jump to the 'personal preferences' category. Because that first assumption needs some thought before we move any further: does it really not matter where you go to church? I guess the question really depends on what you think about God. If God is real, and if He built the church, then don't we first need to ask if God is okay with every church? Let's start there...

Does God Approve of Every Church?

So let's take a few minutes and look through Scripture to see if God approves of every church. If we search the New Testament for God's view of churches, we find that God is *not* pleased with every church; in fact, God says He has no part of churches that continue to disobey His word.

Look, for example, in Revelation chapters 2 and 3. There are a lot of sometimes-confusing symbols in the Book of Revelation, but chapters 2 and 3 are a pretty straightforward look at what Jesus thought about 7 churches in the Roman province of Asia. Jesus is speaking through the apostle John, and what we find out very quickly is that Jesus is not happy with all of the churches that would receive John's letter.

Look first at what He says in Revelation 2:1-7 to the church in the city of Ephesus. He gives them some compliments on good things they are doing, but He also says this in verses 4 and 5:

> *"But I have this against you, that you have left your first love. Therefore remember from where you have fallen, and repent and do the deeds you did at first;*
> *or else I am coming to you and will remove your*

lampstand out of its place – unless you repent."
-Revelation 2:4-5

Jesus is not happy with the Ephesus church because they hadn't been showing love for Christ like they once did. That could mean that they have been disobedient to God in some way, since love and obedience are closely related in Scripture (John 14:15), and since they are told to repent (Revelation 2:5). But whatever it meant, notice what Jesus said would happen if they didn't repent and change: He would "remove their lampstand out of its place." There's some Revelation symbolism, but what does it mean? In Revelation chapters 1-3, the lampstand represents their standing as a church in right relationship with God (see Revelation 1:20). So Jesus was telling them that if they didn't repent, they would no longer be a church that had God's approval.

Wow, so God isn't happy with every church, and churches can lose their relationship with God through continued disobedience. That warning continues several other times in Revelation chapters 2 and 3:

- In Revelation 2:14-16, Jesus tells the church at Pergamum that they will be rejected by God if they don't stop some false teachers who are leading them in the wrong spiritual direction.
- In Revelation 3:1-3, Jesus tells the church at Sardis that they will be rejected by God if they don't wake up spiritually.
- In Revelation 3:15-16, Jesus tells the church at Laodicea that they will be rejected by God ("spit out of His mouth!") if they don't stop their lukewarm, worldly attitudes toward God.

So clearly, God is not happy with every church, and churches can be rejected by God, at least because of disobedience, false teaching, spiritual dullness, or worldly disinterest toward God. Wow, why doesn't our religious world tell us this?

Another passage we would want to notice if we were trying to see if God cared where we went to church: 1 Corinthians 11:17. The Corinthian church had a lot of questions and a lot of problems, and Paul wrote the letter of 1 Corinthians to try to help them straighten out the things they needed to change. (Notice, by the way, that God wanted them to change what they weren't doing right; God *did* care what they taught and practiced!) One of the things they needed to change was how they were worshiping, and Paul discusses how they were messing up the Lord's Supper in 1 Corinthians chapter 11. He begins this section by saying this in verse 17:

> *"But in giving this instruction, I do not praise you, because you come together not for the better but for the worse."*

What?! Paul says that their coming together to worship was actually making them "worse!" I thought it didn't matter where you went to church, that as long as you went it was better than nothing. Apparently not for the Corinthians; their worship assembly was dishonoring God, and because of that, they were making each other spiritually worse by their church services.

The answer wasn't to stop going to church, of course, the answer was to start doing things right - God's way - as Paul went on to teach them. But if they refused? Later in the letter, Paul warned that what he was writing was "the Lord's commandment," and that whoever refused to listen to it would no longer be "recognized" as right with God (1 Corinthians 14:37-38).

More Than A Name

Clearly, God takes church more seriously than our fractured religious world does. Our world says just go to church anywhere you want, it doesn't matter. But as we just saw, the Bible shows that if a church continues to disobey God's word, or continues to teach false doctrines, or continues to worship in ways that dishonor God, they risk losing their right relationship with God.

And I guess it makes sense that just because a group calls itself a church, that doesn't make it right with God. After all, the Bible is clear that just because you claim to be a Christian, that doesn't make you a Christian (see Matthew 7:21-27, for example). We've probably all known people like that. And if it's possible for one person to claim to be a Christian but not be right with God because of their disobedient life, it makes sense that it's possible for a whole group of people to claim to be a church but not be right with God because of their disobedience.

So it's not popular to say, and quite honestly it's not fun to say either, but I think it's biblically true: God does care about what churches do and teach, and not every "church" is acceptable to Him. Just because it is called a church doesn't mean I should be part of it. I need to make sure it's a church that pleases God first.

What a Church Should Be

So we come back to that difficult question David was asking himself at the beginning of this chapter: how do I choose a church? Well, I hope this brief biblical study has made clear that as we begin looking around at churches, the first and most important question we must ask ourselves is whether this church is obeying God's plan or not. Are they teaching God's truth as it is found in Scripture? Are they doing things like worship in the ways God wants? Once we have determined which church or churches are teaching and doing things God's way, *then* we can begin thinking about personal preferences such as where we meet friends or where we think we can best get involved in the programs. But faithfulness to God is the first essential element of a church. If God isn't pleased with what a church is doing, it doesn't matter how great we think they are in other ways, because pleasing God is the most important priority.

There's one more difficulty we need to address before ending this chapter: are we saying that we must find a perfect church to be part of? Obviously not! The church is made up of people, who are all sinful (Romans 3:23, 1 Timothy 1:15), and therefore no church will be perfect, because it is made up of imperfect people.

So someone asks: if all churches are imperfect, then why does it matter which church I am part of? The answer: because from what we've seen in the Bible in this chapter, there is a big difference between:

- a church that falls short while genuinely trying to pursue God's goals to the best of their ability
- a church that stubbornly continues to pursue selfish or sinful goals above faithfulness to God's plan.

Everyone is going to fall short, but sometimes churches stop aiming for what God wants them to aim for. They adopt a teaching or practice that dishonors God because it is against His will, and they have no plans to change it. And when a church persistently allows its goals, or teachings, or worship, or practices to remain different than God's, its spiritual compass is no longer pointing toward God. As we've seen, that's what was happening to the church at Ephesus in Revelation and the church at Corinth in 1 Corinthians: they were drifting away from God in their goals, without intending to change and make it right, and if they didn't wake up and begin to make those changes, they would become a church that was no longer right with God. It wasn't just that they were falling short of God's plan, it was that they had stopped pursuing God's plan and had begun pursuing their own.

So as you're looking for a church home, don't look for perfection. (You won't find it!) But don't settle for a church that has allowed its own goals to take the place of God's goals for His church in their teaching or practice – no matter how popular or friendly or "relevant" they may seem, remember that faithfully pursuing God's plan is priority number one for His church. Even if people are cheering a church, if God is not pleased, that church has failed. To be sure you are worshiping and serving with a church that God is pleased with, make sure that church is striving for the same goals God has for His church in teaching and practice.

The Church of Christ

In churches of Christ, our goal is to make sure we keep our compass pointed in the direction of pleasing God first. It's His church, so we must try to make it what He wanted it to be, whether it's popular or not. We know we are not perfect, but we'd like to think we have the right goals: goals of teaching what God wants to be taught and doing what God wants His church to be doing. We pray that everyone who desires to follow Christ will join us in keeping faithfulness to God as the first, essential priority of His church.

What's Next...

If this chapter has shown us anything, it has reminded us that God is serious about His church! Ever since the first century, there has always been the danger that a church will stop holding up God's goals and begin pursuing their own. So we must constantly be checking our church's "compass" to be sure its goals, teachings, and practices stay pointed in God's direction. How do we do that? Well, the best way I know of is to make sure the church has a spirit you will often hear about in churches of Christ: one we call "restoration." Restoration is a powerful biblical idea that our divided religious world desperately needs to adopt. It's a mindset that has been part of faithful people of God for thousands of years, and it must be part of the church's DNA today as well. What does it mean? Well that's the idea we will explore starting in chapter 4...

Discussion Questions

1) Is there any evidence in the Bible that what a church teaches and practices matters to God? What New Testament examples did we see in this chapter?
2) So if someone you know is looking for a church home, what advice would you give them? What's the most important thing you think they should look for?
3) Is it wrong to let 'personal preferences' play a role in choosing a church home? What are some 'personal preferences' you think would be acceptable to consider, after meeting the criteria of being a faithful church?

4) Do you think there is such a thing as a perfect church? The Jerusalem church in Acts was established by the inspired apostles, and they did some great things, but were they perfect? (Read Acts 5:1-11 and Acts 6:1 for examples of some of their problems.) What does that tell us about our own churches today – should we expect perfection?
5) Even if the sinfulness of man means there is not a perfect church, is there still a perfect *plan* for the church?
6) How can a church be sure it is holding up the perfect plan in spite of our shortcomings? One thought to help: might it include how we respond to our shortcomings? How did the church in Acts respond to its problems? How does this compare to how the church in Ephesus (Rev. 2:1-7) or Pergamum (Rev. 2:14-15) had responded to their shortcomings before John wrote the Book of Revelation to them?

Personal Reflection

1) As we've seen in this chapter, it's possible for churches to stubbornly drift away from following God's plan. Sometimes we do that as individual Christians as well. Read John 14:15. If I'm choosing a sinful lifestyle or a self-centered decision over what God says, what does John 14:15 tell me the root problem may be? What could we do to work on that root problem?
2) Just as there is no such thing as a perfect church, there is also no such thing as a perfect Christian. So what's the difference between a Christian who is

simply falling short and a Christian who has left God? This is a tough question, but perhaps passages like 2 Peter 2:20-22 and Hebrews 10:26-29 can help. As we saw in discussion question number 6 above, might it have something to do with our attitude toward our sins? What has your attitude been toward your sins recently?

3) Sometimes we get caught up in wanting to be part of the trendy or popular group, and sometimes we get caught up in wanting to be part of the trendy or popular church as well. Am I ever tempted to think that human applause is the same as God's approval? If it were necessary, would I be willing to be part of a less-popular church in order to be in a church home that is more faithful to God's plan? Some people today struggle with that!

Section 2: Getting Back To God’s Plan for His Church

CHAPTER 4

Restoring God's Plan For His Church

"So brethren, stand firm and hold to the traditions which you were taught, whether by word of mouth or by letter from us."
-Paul, in 2 Thessalonians 2:15

Starters

- Have you ever seen someone work at restoring an old car or an old house? Why would they do that? What are some steps they would need to take to restore something?
- Name some different reactions people have when they mess something up. What do you think is the best response when we see we have gotten off track?
- Have you ever heard of the "Restoration Movement?" If so, how would you describe it to a friend? If you have not heard of it, any guesses what it might be?

Restoring the House

Jessica couldn't help but be excited as she and her husband pulled into the mostly-dirt driveway. She stopped the car for a second, allowing them both a moment to get a full look at the house they had just bought. To most people, this house had to look like a disappointing purchase. The siding on the house used to be white, but it was now a dirty, faded brownish-color. The front yard was overgrown, and didn't look like it had been cut for months, or longer. The porch was missing a few boards. A few window shutters were broken, hanging at awkward angles. It would have been easy to dismiss this house as too old and broken.

But while many people would have looked at the house and frowned, Jessica and her husband looked at each other with a smile. You see, this old farm house was built decades ago by Jessica's grandparents. She had great memories of sitting on the porch swing sipping tea and watching sunsets with her grandfather; of helping her grandmother cook breakfast; of running around the small farm with her brothers and cousins. After her grandparents had passed away, someone else had bought the place, and it had fallen into disrepair. Now, years later, Jessica and her family were moving back to her hometown, and they found out the old house was for sale. Her husband was doubtful at first, but after hearing how special this place was to Jessica, and after walking around the place and seeing how beautiful it would be if it were fixed up, he was convinced. They bought the house and farm, and began making their to-do list, a plan of action that started today.

They felt like they were on a mission. They pulled the car forward, parked, and began unloading paint, wood, and tools. Jessica's grandparents had built a beautiful house.

Time and poor management had caused it to lose its charm and beauty. Now Jessica and her husband were here to restore it. They already knew that in a short time, everyone would see how beautiful this place was, and they couldn't wait to celebrate as a family when they saw it back the way it should have stayed all along.

Why do you think Jessica is so excited about restoring this house? What are the steps they need take to restore it? Restoration is an exciting idea: from restoring houses to restoring cars to restoring relationships, restoration implies a new beginning of bringing back glory that was lost but can be found again. I hope that by the end of this chapter, we will see the importance of restoring God's plan for His church as well, and re-commit ourselves to that mission. Our first question: why might that be necessary?

Restoring...the Church?

If you spend much time around churches of Christ, you may hear people talk about "restoring the church." What does that mean? Well, the Restoration Movement was a movement that began in the early 1800's and continues today. It began with people who looked around and saw that their religious world was divided, and not only divided, but full of teachings and practices that were not part of God's plan for His church as found in the Bible. God's plan for His church had fallen into disrepair over time. They could have just ignored all the problems, like most people did. But instead, they decided that God's way is the right way, no matter how much effort it takes, and so they summoned the courage to try to restore God's plan to His church. They often began new congregations as undenominational churches, committed only to Jesus Christ and His word – not to a man-made creed or denomination. Many of them took the descriptive name "Church of Christ" to show their allegiance to Christ alone, a description that continues in many of those congregations today.

People from all denominational backgrounds heard about the message of unity and faithfulness based on simply being undenominational Christians, and many left their denominations in order to better pursue God's original plan for His church. Even today, whenever people see that God's plan for His church is not being followed in the religious world, many make the commitment to join that goal of trying to make the church what God intended it to be.

Why would people do that? I mean, it takes a lot of courage to challenge the status quo of religious traditions! People get really upset if someone suggests that a certain religious group isn't following God's plan the way they should – even if it's true. So why would people put so much on the line to restore God's plan? Well, like the example of Jessica and her grandparents' house above, it starts with a genuine love for the original plan, a belief that the original way was the best way. If we love God and the church He built, we will want the church to be what God wants it to be, not just what people want it to be. And if we believe God's way is right, we must find the courage to pursue what is right, no matter the cost.

As you can probably already see, the idea of restoration goes much further back than the 1800's. Whether we know anything about the Restoration Movement or not, what we do need to know is that the idea of "restoration" is built on 2 simple ideas that have their roots in Scripture:

- God has given a plan for His church, a plan that was not supposed to be changed.

- Whenever we find that our teaching or practice is different from God's plan, *we* must change.

Simple, right? Simple yet essential, and sadly missed by much of our religious world. Let's explore those two ideas...

Was God's Plan for the Church Ever Supposed to Change?

Let's look at the first idea: did God really give a plan for His church, one that was supposed to never change? Look first at Jude 3, part of a short letter written by the brother of Jesus:

> *"Beloved, while I was making every effort to write you about our common salvation, I felt the necessity to write you appealing that you contend earnestly for* ***the faith which was once for all handed down to the saints.****"*

Notice the phrase I put in bold. In this passage, "the faith" refers to the teaching and practice that God gave to His church. And how long was "the faith" supposed to last? Jude says it was "once for all" handed to the church. God was never again going to change the teaching and practice of His people! What He gave through the inspired apostles was the one and only plan. It wouldn't change as culture changed. It wouldn't change if people decided they liked something better or made the mistake of thinking they could improve God's plan.

Speaking of that, we might be tempted to forget: the plan for what the church teaches and does was given by the eternal, all-knowing God. He knew the ways in which the world would and wouldn't change. He gave teachings that were true and that would always be true. He gave practices that would build and deepen faith, for all people of all time.

Let's not make the mistake of thinking we can somehow improve God's plan for His church. He gave the plan "once for all," and it is exactly what it needs to be.

Look also at some of the words of the apostle Paul, which teach us that Christians were always supposed to follow the teaching and example of the inspired apostles:

"The things you have learned and received
and heard and seen in me, practice these things,
and the God of peace will be with you."
-Paul, in Philippians 4:9

"Brethren, join in following my example, and observe
those who walk according to the pattern you have in us."
-Paul, in Philippians 3:17

"But even if we, or an angel from heaven,
should preach to you a gospel contrary to what
we have preached to you, he is to be accursed."
-Paul, in Galatians 1:8

"So brethren, stand firm and hold to the traditions
which you were taught, whether by word of mouth
or by letter from us."
-Paul, in 2 Thessalonians 2:15

All four of those verses (and others like them) teach that Christians should follow what was given and taught through the apostles. Notice again that last one, 2 Thessalonians 2:15: we are to "stand firm and hold to the traditions" given by the apostles. God's plan wasn't supposed to change over time. The truth would always be the truth. God knew technology and culture would change, but God had the eternal perspective to know what faith-teachings and faith-practices would best build up our souls, in every place and every time. So our standard today is the same as it was in the Bible: we should be teaching and practicing what the apostles taught and practiced.

Who Should Change When It's Off?

So the first biblical idea of restoration is that God has given His eternal plan for His church through the apostles, and therefore the church's teaching and practice weren't supposed to change. Let's look at the second idea: whenever we find that we are teaching or practicing something different from God's plan, *we* are the ones who should change.

Would you agree that it's possible for people to mess up God's plan for the church? If we humans have proved anything, we've proved that we are good at messing things up! We can take beautiful farm houses, and over time we can let them fall into disrepair. We can take beautiful rivers and lakes, and over time we can let them become full of pollution and trash. We break things. We spill things. We litter. We have wrecks. We don't take care of things like we should. We take even great advances of technology and we mess up their potential, using technology to hurt people, through things like killing with advanced weapons or stealing digital information. Sometimes we do it on purpose and sometimes we don't, but either way, we can mess things up with the best of them.

We have seen in these first three chapters that the church was built by Christ and is important to God. Surely humans couldn't mess up the church, could we? Of course we can, that's what we do! In fact, the New Testament predicted that man's teachings would pull people away from God's plan for His church. Look at a couple of passages:

> *"But the Spirit explicitly says that in later times some will fall away from the faith, paying attention to*

deceitful spirits and doctrines of demons,"
-The apostle Paul, in 1 Timothy 4:1

"Preach the word...For the time will come when they will not endure sound doctrine; but wanting to have their ears tickled, they will accumulate for themselves teachers in accordance with their own desires, and will turn away their ears from the truth and will turn aside to myths."
-The apostle Paul, in 2 Timothy 4:2-4

These verses (and others like them) show that God knew there would always be false ideas and false teachings, and that many people would end up following human ideas rather than God's teaching for Christian living and for His church. History shows us that human ideas have indeed led people down paths that took people away from God's plan for His church. As the generations after the apostles went on, all sorts of things were taught that were not part of God's plan: denominations, creeds, war crusades, people declaring their own authority over God's church, different teachings on salvation, different teachings on worship. That list could go on for a long time.

So what should we do whenever we realize that we are not following the plan God gave His church? We work to restore God's plan! We don't shrug and say "oh well, there's nothing I can do about it." We don't make excuses for keeping things as they are. We don't remain disobedient and tell God it's His job to overlook our willful disobedience. Instead, we do what people of sincere faith have always done: we change to try to line up more with God's plan. Sometimes that's easy and sometimes it's difficult, but the Christian life is a life of allowing ourselves to be transformed into what God wants. Sometimes we must do that with the church. It's not God's job to change His plan to let us do what we want;

it's our job to change our actions in order to follow God's perfect plan.

The Ongoing Task of Restoration

So the big goal of this chapter is to emphasize the simple truth of those 2 biblical foundations, foundations that produce within us a spirit of restoration:

- God has given a plan for His church, a plan that was not supposed to be changed.
- Whenever we find that our teaching or practice is different from God's plan, *we* must change.

So when will we be finished restoring God's plan? Well, since we are all sinful people (Rom 3:23), and since we don't have the perfect knowledge God has (Isa. 55:8-9), restoration will need to be an ongoing process in our lives and in our churches. To keep that process alive, we must develop constant attitudes of reflection, humility, and courage. The importance of reflection: we must keep our eyes open to see what we might need to change, in case we've missed something that God wants us to teach or practice. The importance of humility: if we find something we need to change, we must have the humility to admit that we need to do better. The importance of courage: we must have the courage to take whatever steps are necessary to align ourselves with God's plan.

Keeping the principle of restoration alive in our faith is what helps the church remain faithful to God. We will likely never be perfect in our lives or our churches, but we must be faithful. As we saw in the last chapter, God rejects churches that have stopped pursuing faithfulness to His plan. Staying faithful means constantly listening to God and changing whenever we see that we have fallen short.

The Church of Christ

Will you join us in keeping a spirit of restoration alive among God's people? In striving to simply be Christians, desiring to please God above all else, we are trying to keep that mentality of reflection, humility, and courage. Let's never settle for allowing God's church to remain in disrepair. Let's never allow the mistakes of history – or the modern day attempts to "improve" what God designed – to become permanent obstacles that hold the church back from God's eternal plan. Starting with ourselves, let's work to restore all that we can in God's plan for His church, trusting He knows what is best for His people.

What's Next...

So what needs to be restored today? In the next few chapters, we will see some starting points, exploring several areas of modern-day religion that we believe need to be restored back to what God intended. If we could make these changes, we would go a long way towards helping the church look more like God wants it to look. Changing some of these things would probably be unpopular, but that's the choice we often make as people of God: am I willing to do what's right for God, even if the world doesn't like it? Will I trust that God's way really is the right way? That's the kind of courage and trust God wants us to have...

Discussion Questions

1) In the example at the beginning of the chapter, of Jessica restoring the farm house, why do you think Jessica is so excited about restoring this particular house? What role does love play? How might her

motives be similar to our motives in wanting to restore God's plan for His church?

2) What are the steps Jessica and her husband would need to take to restore the farm house? How might those steps be similar to the steps we would need to take to restore God's plan for His church?
3) What are the two biblical principles that make up the idea of restoration?
4) What are some passages that show God's plan for His church was never supposed to change?
5) Why might people think that it's OK to change God's plan for His church? If we think we can improve God's plan for His church, what might we be forgetting about God?
6) When we see that the church is teaching or doing something differently from God's plan, what should we do? What other options are there? Why might people choose the other options?
7) Do you think restoration of God's plan for the church is a never-ending process? Why or why not?
8) What qualities are required for us to keep a constant spirit of restoration in our lives and our churches?
9) Do you think a widespread effort to restore God's plan for His church would be well-accepted by most of the religious world? Why or why not?

Personal Reflection

1) Imagine you lived in the early 1800's like some of America's "Restoration Movement" leaders, and you have been reading your Bible. You realize that God wants His people to be undenominational, and yet

everyone around you is divided into denominational groups. You realize God has a certain teaching and practice for His church, and yet you don't know any church that is following it. What do you think you would have done? What do you think most people would have done?

2) What if your church found that they were doing something different from God's plan for His church? How would God hope everyone would respond?

3) We said that restoration requires an ongoing attitude of reflection, humility, and courage. Which of those do you think is most difficult for people: making time to reflect, humility to admit wrong, or courage to change? Which is most difficult for you personally?

CHAPTER 5

Restoring God's Plan For Scripture

"All Scripture is inspired by God and profitable for teaching, for reproof, for correction, for training in righteousness;"
- 2 Timothy 3:16

Starters

- Brainstorm a list of things that people listen to for their religious ideas. It can include different religious books or religious leaders. Why do you think they trust those things?
- Should we trust people's ideas when it comes to God and faith and eternity? Why or why not?
- Do you know what a denominational creed book is? Why do religious groups have creed books or handbooks? Do you see any dangers in a church having a creed book or handbook?

- Does the Bible claim to be from God? If that's true, how should that affect the church's attitude toward it?

The Christian Book

If someone were to come up and ask you to name the book of the Christian faith, what would you say? I hope you would say, "the Bible." I think most people would. In fact, you could probably go ask 100 people on the street this week to name the book of the Christian faith, and my guess is all 100 would say the Bible. If you asked them to name the book of the Muslim faith, they would say the Koran. If you asked for the book of the Mormon faith, they would say the Book of Mormon. But for Christianity, almost everyone agrees the Bible is the place to look.

In the last chapter we saw that we must develop a spirit of restoration in the church: an attitude of looking for where we may have messed up God's plan, and having the commitment to change to better do and teach things God's way. So the next question naturally follows: how do I know what God's plan is for my life as a Christian and for His church? That's where our religious world makes it difficult. You would think that it would be common sense for Christians to look to the Bible for answers about what they should believe and practice. Unfortunately, our divided religious world has become accustomed to looking to many different places for answers.

A young lady goes to ask her preacher a question about why their church believes something, and instead of looking at the Bible, he begins talking about what their denominational handbook says. A visitor asks a leader at another church about why they practice certain things, and he begins talking about creeds that humans put together many years after the Bible, or what a church council said they should believe. Knowing the Bible is the book of the Christian faith, the ones hearing the handbook and creed book answers must have another question in the back of their minds: why aren't we looking at the Bible for answers?

That's a great question for today's religious world: why aren't we looking at the Bible for answers? We have so many people following denominational creed books, each one with different teachings, each one setting itself up as an authority to be followed. We have many in the religious world following religious leaders, many of whom set themselves up as the authority, encouraging people to follow their personal teachings or their new and trendy ideas. Some people want to simply follow their church or family traditions. Some people are just doing whatever they personally want to be right.

What's the real standard of authority for God's church? I hope this chapter reaffirms that God's word as found in the Bible is the authority – and the only authority – for God's church. That's how God intended Scripture to function, and it's up to us to let people know that creed books and people's ideas and religious traditions are not real authorities when it comes to the church. If we love God enough to try to get back to His plan for the church, we must make sure we know where to find His plan! That may seem like common sense, but I think our experience shows that many people listen to other 'authorities' far more than they should.

The Danger of Creeds and Handbooks

Someone asks, 'Why are creed books such a bad thing?' Let me tell a true story to illustrate. Recently, in one of America's larger and most religious cities, there was a large denominational church that was led by a 'pastor,' just as their denominational creed taught. To his credit, this pastor began reading his Bible, and he found that in the New Testament, churches were not led by a preacher, and that preachers were not the same thing as pastors. He found that the pastors were a group of men, often called elders, with certain qualifications, and these elders had spiritual authority over the congregation. He was surprised to find that the preacher wasn't supposed to be in charge of the church as his denomination taught. (If you haven't studied this before, we will have more on the topic of church leadership in chapter 7.)

What's more, this pastor was so honest-hearted with Scripture that he began teaching what he found in the New Testament to the congregation. He encouraged them to do it the Bible's way: to appoint elders to lead the congregation, and to have the preacher simply be a preacher, not the authority over the church. He taught, and the church debated. Some agreed, some didn't. Well, they had to put this 'new teaching' up for a vote, because – guess why? – that's what the handbook said you had to do. Would they vote for the Bible's form of leadership, or for the denomination's traditional teaching? When the congregation's votes were counted, the winning side voted to keep things the denomination's way: the preacher would still be a 'pastor,' and he would be in charge, just like the handbook taught.

Think about that for a second. Someone found in Scripture how God wanted His church to do things. They found that it was different than what they had always done. This group of people trying to follow God had the choice: do we want to do it God's way, or keep it the way the creed says? In the end, the creed was allowed to speak louder than Scripture. God's way was pushed aside.

And that, in a nutshell, is the problem with creeds or handbooks or man-made traditions: when we allow them to be an authority, they begin to drown out the voice of Scripture, and we have started trying to live up to the wrong standard. The goal of Christianity is not to do what the creed book says, or what man-made tradition says, or what any individual person says. The goal is to do things God's way – it's His church! It's time we throw away our creeds and handbooks and anything that allows itself to be a rival to God's word. The only authority that must be trusted and followed is the one that comes straight from God: the Bible.

Let's Remember What We're Talking About

Why is the Bible the authority for the church? Because Scripture is the only place that we find the clear words of God.

Notice the classic description of Scripture in 2 Timothy 3:16:

> *"**All Scripture is inspired by God** and profitable for teaching, for reproof, for correction, for training in righteousness;"*
> *-The apostle Paul to Timothy, in 2 Timothy 3:16*

The word we translate "inspired" literally means "God-breathed." God breathed the words through the authors as they were written down in the Bible. There are many good writings in the world that are well worth reading, but the

Bible holds the only words we have that were "God-breathed" through men inspired by the Holy Spirit.

After Jesus sent the Holy Spirit into His apostles (see John 16:13 and Acts 2:33), God spoke His words through them. So whenever the apostles taught and wrote about Christianity, they were giving the words of God about Christ and about His church. We have their writings in our New Testament, and Christians recognized that their words were the words of God. Look at the following passages:

"For this reason we also constantly thank God that when
you received the word of God which you heard from us,
you accepted it not as the word of men,
but for what it really is, the word of God,
which also performs its work in you who believe."
-The apostle Paul, in 1 Thessalonians 2:13.

"If anyone thinks he is a prophet or spiritual, let him
recognize that the things which I write to you are the
Lord's commandment. But if anyone does
not recognize this, he is not recognized."
-The apostle Paul, in 1 Corinthians 14:37-38

Someone might say, "Well, just because it claims to be God's word doesn't mean it is." And that's exactly right. But I'd encourage you to take some time and study further why Christians have always believed that the Bible has all the evidences of being from God. I think you'll find that Scripture has given prophecies and predictions that have been fulfilled in history with an accuracy that humans simply can't match. I think you'll find that Scripture contains many geographical and historical facts, and that those facts have been found correct as far as evidence can test them. I think you will find that Scripture presents the world in a way that resonates with what we see: the struggle of good and evil, in a temporary world where we sense there is something bigger and better beyond it. For these and many other reasons, I believe you will find that Scripture not only claims to be from God, but bears the marks of actually being from God.

And not only does Scripture show the marks of being inspired by God as it claims, but Scripture makes it clear that we must listen to God's word above any other source of ideas. After all, Scripture is the only source that we know comes from God! Let's look at what Scripture says about all the other "voices" that try to give us religious direction...

What Scripture Says About All the Other Options

1) Visions? What if someone claims to have received a vision from God? If they say that their vision commanded them to teach or do something different from Scripture, should we listen to the vision? Well, my first question would be: how do you know that the vision was from God? There are several different things that can lead people to think they are having a vision, and not all of those things are from God. (Look at 1 John 4:1, by the way, which tells us that not every "spirit" comes from God!) God gives us a great measuring stick for whether or not we should listen to a claim of a 'vision:'

> *"But even if we, or an angel from heaven, should preach to you a gospel contrary to what we have preached to you, he is to be accursed! As we have said before, so I say again now, if any man is preaching to you a gospel contrary to what you received, he is to be accursed!"*
> *-Paul, in Galatians 1:8-9*

What would you think if an angel appeared to you and told you to do something different from the teachings of the New Testament? Would you listen? The Bible says don't listen to anything different from the New Testament gospel, even if you felt an angel or a vision came to you. Some entire religions have been built on claims that an angel gave a 'new message.' The Bible says that message should not have been accepted if it was different from Scripture.

2) Man-made Traditions? "Our church has always done it this way." Or "our denomination has always done it that way." Should man-made tradition be allowed to stand over the word of God? Look at what Jesus said to the Pharisees:

"But in vain do they worship Me,
Teaching as doctrines the precepts of men.'
Neglecting the commandment of God,
you hold to the tradition of men."
He was also saying to them,
"You are experts at setting aside the commandment
of God in order to keep your tradition."
-Jesus, in Mark 7:7-9

The Pharisees had created their own special tradition, a hand-washing ceremony that they taught was necessary. When Jesus didn't practice it, they got upset at Him, and Jesus told them that putting tradition at the same level of God's word is wrong. We must never let man's traditions take the place of following God's word!

3) Our feelings? Some people think, "Shouldn't I just follow my feelings in religion?" "Surely my heart won't lead me astray." "Just do what feels right." Unfortunately, our feelings are not the same thing as God's word. In fact, since we are all affected by sin, our feelings can often point us in the wrong direction! Look at this passage:

"He who trusts in his own heart is a fool,
But he who walks wisely will be delivered."
-Proverbs 28:26

Jeremiah 17:9 also reminds us how sin can make our heart untrustworthy, saying, "The heart is more deceitful than all else." My heart only tells me what I want, which can often be self-serving and sinful. My heart can get filled with ideas from bad sources that affect it the wrong way. Our hearts and our feelings are not trustworthy sources for deciding what is right; God's word is the truth that is unaffected by the unstable ups and downs of our hearts.

4) My conscience? God gave us a conscience, which helps encourage us to do what we believe is right. But our conscience is not a fool-proof guide, because the conscience must be trained to truly know what is right and wrong. Before he became a Christian, Paul was killing Christians because he believed it was the right thing to do, and so killing Christians didn't violate his conscience. (Read Acts 23:1, where Paul says he had always lived in good conscience.) Since killing Christians didn't violate Paul's conscience, did that make it right? Of course not! Our conscience must be taught the truth and trained to understand right and wrong properly.

"There is a way which seems right to a man,
But its end is the way of death."
-Proverbs 16:25

Conscience is a blessing from God, but the conscience must be trained in God's truth. Don't trust your conscience over the word of God. Instead, first let the word of God reshape your conscience.

5) My culture? All of us are affected by our culture, and every culture has ideas in it that are different from God's truth. There are some things people will hear their entire life in media, and when they hear something different in Scripture, they are tempted to think Scripture must be wrong. This is especially true in our American culture, where we seem to think that our technology and media power have given us the ability to make the rules on morals and the spiritual world. Let's not forget that God sees things from a higher place than our culture does!

"For My thoughts are not your thoughts,
Nor are your ways My ways," declares the Lord.
"For as the heavens are higher than the earth,
So are My ways higher than your ways
And My thoughts than your thoughts."
-Isaiah 55:8-9

Our culture (like every culture) will see some things differently from Scripture's truth. Let's not forget that the eternal, all-wise God can see things more clearly than we can, even if we don't understand them right now in our sin-blinded world. One of Satan's favorite tactics is to make something that is wrong appear right, and to make what is right appear wrong (see Isaiah 5:20, 2 Corinthians 4:4, 11:14). We must trust God's word over whatever the shifting ideas of culture happen to think is right at this particular moment in time.

6) Any other options? I hope the point is clear: Scripture is inspired by God, and God tells us in Scripture not to listen to anything else that is different from what it teaches. The Christian truth was never going to change (read Jude 3 again), and the word of Christ is what's going to judge us in the last day:

"He who rejects Me and does not receive My sayings,
has one who judges him; the word I spoke is
what will judge him at the last day."
-Jesus, in John 12:48

You and I will be judged by God's word. We won't be judged by whether we followed what the creed book said, or whether we followed what our preacher said. We will be judged by God's word. So no matter how nice or sincere the preacher or handbook writers might be, I want to know what God has to say in Scripture, and I'm going to trust Scripture over every other voice.

Rediscovering Scripture

One of the Bible's great revivals is the Old Testament revival of King Josiah in 2 Kings chapters 22 and 23. God's temple in Jerusalem had fallen into disrepair, and so Josiah told the high priest to count whatever money they had in the temple, so they could pay workmen to fix it up. As Hilkiah the high priest was organizing the money, a curious thing happened: he found the book of God's law in the temple (2 Kings 22:8). I have no idea how everyone had lost God's law. I suppose they had just continued doing religious things, but somewhere along the way God's word had been so underused that it simply got lost.

What happened next is special. They read the word of God, and they brought it to King Josiah to let him hear it also. As he heard the words of Scripture, King Josiah realized that they were not doing things the way they were supposed to do them. Do you know what he did? He didn't say "oh well, let's just keep the traditions the way we've done them, it doesn't matter what Scripture says." He didn't say "I hear what it says, but I just like our way better." King Josiah had a humble heart before God, and so he begged God's forgiveness for their sins and their ignorance, and he committed himself to restoring God's plans for His people (which in Josiah's time was the Old Testament laws given through Moses centuries earlier). Josiah gathered Israel together and had God's word read to them, and they all realized the same thing: we've been doing things wrong. The entire nation committed itself to changing, and they began a great revival of throwing out idols and restoring the true service of God again.

What started such a special revival and restoration of God's plan? They rediscovered the word of God. If we want a revival in our religious world, a revival of breaking down denominational walls and man-made teachings and all the other things that have messed up God's plan over the centuries since Jesus built His church, we need to start by rediscovering the word of God. When we put Scripture where it belongs – as the only religious authority for teaching and practice – we have taken the first big step toward restoring the church to what it was supposed to be.

The Church of Christ

In the churches of Christ, we claim no creed or authority besides Scripture itself. There is no handbook to follow besides the Bible. There is no tradition that we refuse to change if we find that it is different from Scripture. We seek to read the word of God and practice what it says. Man-made creeds and traditions block people from seeing God's truth, and it's long past time that we took their imagined authority away. Once we let man's ideas stand alongside God's, we begin polluting the truth and we begin going off course again. That's what man has always done, but God wants His church to be faithful to His eternal word alone.

And here's the magic of taking Scripture as our only authority: not only is it the right thing to do, but it also has a self-correcting mechanism. What does that mean? Well, when Scripture is your only goal, it is easier to change whenever you find something that you might have missed. There is no set-in-stone creed blocking the view. No votes are necessary. We're just trying to follow the Bible, so if we find something in the Bible that we've been messing up, we simply begin working on doing better at whatever we've missed. If we find in the Bible that we've been teaching salvation wrong, we change our teaching in order to follow the Bible better. If we find that we've been organizing our church leadership wrong, we change our form of leadership in order to follow God's word better. Simple, right? But that's almost impossible to do if we let man-made creeds and teachings have any authority. The self-correcting mechanism of following "Scripture only" is a powerful tool for constant renewal and restoration in God's people.

Will you join us in making Scripture the only religious authority in your life and in God's church? We encourage everyone to read and study the Bible for themselves. If you find something we are not doing according to Scripture, please let us know, because we want to do it God's way! If you find you or your church have been practicing something that's not from God, prayerfully put your trust in God alone and change! If a faith teaching or practice is not found in the New Testament, then it's on shaky ground. If I'm looking for religious answers, I don't want human ideas or creed books or handbooks. I'd rather plant my faith and practice on God's word, and then I know it's right. Wouldn't you rather do the same? Make sure you are part of a church that listens to Scripture and follows Scripture, and Scripture only. That's what God wants His people to do. Will we have the courage to see past all the man-made stuff and try to simply follow God's word?

What's Next...

Once we've established that Scripture is the only religious authority we can trust, it's time to dig further into Scripture to see some common religious teachings and practices that need to be restored back to what Scripture teaches. We will start with the most important one: what must we do to be saved? Sadly, our religious world has often messed this up, and it's time to start teaching it the way it was taught in Scripture. We'll look at the Scriptures, and let you see it for yourself...

Discussion Questions

1) How do you think people would react if they heard someone teach that we need to throw away all the denominational creed books and just follow the Bible?
2) Besides the Bible, what are some things that people trust in making religious decisions? What does the Bible say about those different options? What makes the Bible worth trusting?
3) Jesus said that the Pharisees were letting their tradition cause disobedience to God's word. Are all traditions bad? (Hint: read 1 Corinthians 11:2 and 2 Thessalonians 2:15, where the "tradition" of the apostles is said to be good.) What makes some traditions good and others bad?

4) Why do people trust their heart in making religious decisions? What's the problem with trusting your heart?
5) Why do people trust their conscience in making religious decisions? What's the problem with trusting conscience alone?
6) Why does our culture often think it knows better than Scripture? Can you think of some ways today that Satan convinces our culture to call "good evil and evil good" (Isa. 5:20)? Why do you believe God can be trusted over the shifting ideas of culture?
7) How does having Scripture as your only standard give a "self-correcting mechanism" to the church? Read Acts 17:11, and think about the humble attitude the Bereans must have had toward God.
8) What started the revival of Josiah? How else could they have reacted when they heard Scripture say they had been doing things wrong? Why do you think they decided to listen to Scripture?

Personal Reflection

1) If revival begins with God's word, like it did in 2 Kings 22-23, I must make sure I'm allowing God's word to keep speaking in my life. How much time have I been spending with God's word lately? Do I have a plan or goal to help me keep spending time with God's word?
2) Why are we tempted to trust culture's ideas so much? How does culture get its message into our heads? What does Philippians 4:8 and Proverbs 4:23

say about the things I need to allow to get into my mind and heart? Am I guarding my heart? How?

3) Are you interested in studying more about why Christians believe Scripture is truly the word of God, just as it claims? Find a good book on "Christian evidences" and explore some of the reasons Christians believe the Bible is something humans could not have put together without God's help.
4) When I see the Bible teaching something different than I've been doing, am I willing to change? Or do I make excuses? How can I make pleasing God my highest goal?

CHAPTER 6

Restoring God's Plan For Teaching How To Be Saved

"Now when they heard this, they were pierced to the heart,
and said to Peter and the rest of the apostles,
'Brethren, what shall we do?'
Peter said to them, 'Repent, and each of you be baptized
in the name of Jesus Christ for the forgiveness of your sins;
and you will receive the gift of the Holy Spirit.'"
- Acts 2:37-38

Starters

- Name some different ways religious groups teach 'how to be saved.' Why do you think there are so many differences in what they teach?
- Do you think it matters which way we follow to be saved? Why or why not?

- Who would you trust to tell you that you are saved? A friend? A preacher? If so, which one and why? A church? If so, which one and why?
- Who ultimately decides (in eternity) whether we are saved or not? How should that answer change people's answers to the questions above?

Who Should We Listen To?

Let's say you never went to church growing up. You go through life just doing what everyone else does – you go to school, you hang out with friends, you have family time, you enjoy your hobbies and life activities. But then at some point you begin thinking about spiritual things. You realize that life feels short and a little empty. You begin thinking that surely there is some bigger purpose and meaning to it all. And so you start asking questions about faith and God, and you begin learning about different religious faiths. As your thoughts come together over time, you are intrigued by Christianity. You discover that it is a thinking faith, and so you find articles and websites that intelligently and kindly explain why Christians believe God is real, the Bible is from God, and Jesus is God's Son. You learn why we need Jesus' sacrifice for our sins on the cross, and you learn about the peace and joy found in forgiveness through Jesus Christ alone. After a lot of personal reflection, you realize that this is right, and you feel ready to become a Christian.

What is your next step? I've wondered how someone outside of Christianity feels about all the different teachings on how to become a Christian. You might ask one friend who goes to church, and they will say "Just have faith in your heart and you are saved." Another friend says he was baptized as a baby, and then when he was older he went through a ceremony to make his salvation official. Some preachers will say, “Pray this prayer with me and you will be saved.” Another group says, “Have water sprinkled on your head.” Another says, “You will have a feeling in your heart,” or “you will speak in tongues and then you are saved.”

There are enough differences to make you throw your hands up in frustration! How do I become a Christian? What must I do to be saved? You’ve come to the most important commitment of your life, and it’s difficult to know who to listen to. How would you decide what to do?

Well, I think we all agree that the only one who can save us is God. So do you know who I want to listen to on ‘how to be saved?’ God Himself! I don’t want the words of a creed or the promises of a preacher or just what somebody heard somebody say. You may be the nicest and most sincere person in the world, but I don’t want to trust your promises with my salvation, because salvation is God’s gift, not man’s.

If I told you, “Go to the highest mountain near your hometown, bow on your knees, clap your hands above your head three times, shout out your sins, and then whisper the name of Jesus, you will be saved.” If you did it, would that make you saved? Or if I said, “If you will do 5 good deeds to random strangers for 5 days, you will be saved.” If you did it, would that make you saved? You see where I’m going with this. If you did what I told you to do, you would only have my promises on your salvation. Unfortunately for you, I am not God, and I don’t get to hand out tickets for salvation and heaven. That’s God’s place. And so it only makes sense to let God – and God alone – tell us how to receive His salvation. I want to hear ‘how to be saved’ from God Himself, and when I do it His way, I will know that I have His salvation and His promises.

What Does the Bible Say?

So I hope we agree: the promises of men can't really give salvation. The only way to teach salvation is to make sure we teach the words and promises of God. As we saw in the last chapter, that means going to the New Testament and seeing what the Bible says about how God wanted His church to teach salvation. So the question becomes: what does God say?

Let's start by looking at the words of Jesus while He was on earth, and then we will see what His inspired apostles taught after He returned to heaven. What did Jesus say must be done to be saved?

- **Jesus said we must believe in Him to be saved.** *"Therefore I said to you that you will die in your sins; for unless you believe that I am He, you will die in your sins."* -Jesus, in John 8.24.

  What does it mean when Jesus says we must believe that He is "He?" It means we must believe that He is the Christ, the Son of God (Matthew 16:16), and that He is the only way to salvation (John 14:6).

- **Jesus said we must repent of our sins to be saved.** *"I tell you, no, but unless you repent, you will all likewise perish."* -Jesus, in Luke 13:3.

  What does it mean to "repent?" The word literally means to "change your mind." So when we repent, we decide in our minds to stop following sin, and to start living according to the teachings of God. Getting sin out of your life will be a lifelong process, but "repentance" is a sincere commitment of the mind to change directions back toward God.

- **Jesus said we must be baptized to be saved.** *"Jesus answered, "Truly, truly, I say to you, unless one is born of water and the Spirit he cannot enter into the kingdom of God."* -Jesus, in John 3:5

  What does "born of water" mean? Well, in the chapters around that verse, John the Baptist has been baptizing people in water (John 1:24-28) and Jesus is teaching people to be baptized in water also (John 3:26, John 4:1). When Jesus said we must be "born of water," He was talking about baptism. He said it even more clearly at the end of His ministry, when He told the apostles how to teach others to become followers of Jesus: *"Go therefore and make disciples of all the nations, baptizing them in the name of the Father and the Son and the Holy Spirit,"* (Jesus, in Matthew 28:19).

So Jesus said we must believe, repent, and be baptized to be saved. After Jesus ascended back to the Father, we see His inspired apostles teaching that same message. In Acts chapter 2, Peter preaches about Jesus to thousands of people in Jerusalem. He tells them that Jesus is "Lord and Christ" (Acts 2:36). The crowd is then "pierced to the heart" in verse 37, meaning they believed the message (because with the heart a person believes, according to Romans 10:10). When they believed, what did Peter tell them to do?

> *Peter said to them, "Repent, and each of you be baptized in the name of Jesus Christ for the forgiveness of your sins; and you will receive the gift of the Holy Spirit."*
> *-Acts 2:38*

Believe, repent, and be baptized. Just like Jesus taught! That day, 3000 souls were baptized (Acts 2:41), and the church promised by Jesus had begun. And did you notice what Peter said they would have in that act of baptism? "Forgiveness of sins," and the "gift of the Holy Spirit." When someone believes and repents, they are baptized, and at the point of baptism, God saves them.

As you keep reading your New Testament, you find a couple more details that fill in "how to become a Christian." We find that when people became Christians, they also made a **confession** of their faith that Jesus is Lord, Christ, and Son of God. You see that in passages like Romans 10:9-10, where part of salvation is confessing that "Jesus is Lord." You see it also in 1 Timothy 6:12, where Paul says that Timothy made "the good confession" which was part of receiving "eternal life." Right before I was baptized, our preacher asked me if I believed that Jesus Christ was the Son of God. I answered that I did, and he said "upon that confession of faith, we will now baptize you in the name of the Father, the Son, and the Holy Spirit." Since the Bible shows us confession of faith in Jesus is also part of becoming a Christian, we teach and practice that confession of faith right before baptism.

Some people also point out that in order to have faith in Christ, you must first **hear** about Christ. That's what Paul said in Romans 10:17: "So faith comes from hearing, and hearing through the word of Christ." You can't believe in Jesus if you don't know about Him! Faith in Jesus isn't just a random feeling that comes from nowhere in particular. Faith is built on learning about who Jesus is and what that means for our lives.

So how do you become a Christian, according to what we've just seen in the New Testament? In churches of Christ, you will often hear people summarize the Bible's teaching this way: *hear, believe, repent, confess, and be baptized*. Those five actions are a good summary of what Jesus and the apostles taught about salvation. And when I've done what God's word says to do, then I know I have the promises of God on my life and my eternity.

Where We've Missed It

Hear, believe, repent, confess, and be baptized. That seems like a good summary to me, and all from the Bible. It would be great if we could just stop right there and say, "Now let's all teach it the way they taught it in the Bible!" But it's not always that easy.

Why is there so much confusion in the religious world about how to be saved? Well, one of the biggest problems, I believe, is when religious groups emphasize some verses and ignore others. And in today's religious world, that problem usually has to do with the issues of faith and baptism. Some groups emphasize all the passages about faith, and they ignore or devalue the passages about baptism. Other groups emphasize the act of baptism, but don't teach that personal faith is necessary for baptism. Let's ask a few questions about some of the things you see in our religious world, and what the Bible says about them.

1) Does the Bible teach that we are saved by faith only?

Some people point to passages that only mention faith for salvation, and they stop there. They do not teach biblical baptism. They will look at passages like Acts 16:31 or Romans 5:1-2, and they point out that faith saves us. They stop there, and don't look at the other passages we saw above about salvation. They may even say that we are saved by "faith only."

But the Bible is clear that "faith only" does not save us. In James 2:19 the Bible says that even the demons believe. Are the demons saved? Of course not, and that's his point. In James 2:24, in fact, the Bible says that "faith alone" does *not* save us! As that passage teaches, "faith without works is dead" (James 2:17,26). Our faith does save us, but not faith alone. We are saved through faith when our faith leads us to respond to God the way God commands, which includes repentance, confession, and baptism.

Another example showing "faith only" doesn't save us is John 12:42-43. There, many of the Jewish leaders "believed in" Jesus, but would not confess Him, because "they loved the approval of men rather than the approval of God." So clearly, they believed, yet they did not have the approval of God because they wouldn't confess Jesus. As Jesus said in Matthew 10:32-33, being willing to confess Jesus in our life is essential if we want to be saved. So just like the demons in James 2, these Jewish leaders are another clear example that one can "have faith" but not be saved. We are not saved by faith only. Faith saves us, but only when it acts, by obeying the way God commands.

2) Does the Bible teach that we are saved by baptism only?

You could look at passages that only mention faith and ignore the others, and you could also look at passages that only mention baptism and ignore the others. For example, 1 Peter 3:21 says that "baptism now saves us." It only mentions baptism, so does that mean faith isn't necessary? Of course not. If we want to let the Bible speak, we must be fair with it and see all that it has to say on the topic of salvation, not just a verse here or there.

But some religious groups practice baptism as if it saves regardless of faith. For example, some groups teach that we should baptize babies to save them, even though the baby has no personal faith of its own. Is that what God wants? There are at least two problems with this teaching. First, baptizing babies misses the Bible's teaching that children are in a saved state until they reach the age where they can make their own choices about right and wrong. (Study Mark 10:13-15 and Isaiah 7:16 for good starting points on that topic.) Second, baptizing babies misses the Bible's teaching that baptism doesn't mean anything to us unless it is done on the basis of our own personal faith. Can we just go around throwing people in the water, whether they have faith or not, and then declare they are saved because they were baptized? Of course not. The Bible teaches that faith and baptism must go together, as we see in Colossians 2:12:

> *"having been buried with Him in **baptism**, in which you were also raised up with Him through **faith** in the working of God, who raised Him from the dead."*

We are raised up with Christ in baptism, but that happens "through faith." We must have our own personal faith for baptism to bring the promises of God.

Baptism doesn't save by itself, but when faith and baptism are united together, look at all the things that God says He does in baptism: makes us a follower of Jesus (Matthew 28:19), forgives our sins (Acts 2:38), causes us to be born again into the kingdom of God (John 3:5), washes our sins away (Acts 22:16), unites us with Christ and His saving death (Romans 6:3-4), gives us a new life (Romans 6:4), clothes us with Christ (Galatians 3:27), puts us into Christ's body the church (1 Corinthians 12:13), saves us (1 Peter 3:21). Those are amazing promises! We are saved by God in baptism, but only when we have faith in Jesus that "raises us up with Him" in baptism (Col. 2:12). Faith and baptism must go together!

3) What about the "Sinner's Prayer?" Many groups today teach that we can be saved by saying a prayer, often described as asking Jesus into our hearts or something similar. Well, as you read through the New Testament, you won't find one single example of someone being saved by a "sinner's prayer." I'm not sure how this human tradition started or how it became so popular in our religious culture, but many sincere people have said a sinner's prayer because a preacher told them to, and they have no idea that the sinner's prayer doesn't come from the Bible. As always, I encourage you to read and search for yourself, but many people even in religious groups that teach the sinner's prayer are starting to notice that it's not in the Bible, and they are beginning to encourage people to stop this teaching. They are right, because God never promises His salvation through a sinner's prayer, and God is the one who decides how we must be saved.

4) What about sprinkling and pouring? We have seen the importance of baptism in God's plan for "how to be saved." We then need to ask the question: what is baptism? Some people sprinkle water over someone's head and call it baptism. Some people pour a certain amount of water and call it baptism. What does the Bible say?

As you read the Bible's descriptions of baptism, it becomes clear that baptism was a full immersion in water. It is described as a "burial" in Romans 6:4 and Colossians 2:12, where it says we are buried with Christ in baptism. Have you ever seen a burial where the body was only sprinkled with a handful of dirt? In a burial, the body is put completely into its burial place. Baptism is a full "burial" in water, which is why descriptions of baptism in the Bible include going down into the water (Acts 8:38) and then coming out of the water (Mark 1:10). Just as Jesus was buried and raised from the dead, we are buried in and raised up from the waters of baptism (Romans 6:3-4). You won't see anyone sprinkled or poured in the New Testament, so God hasn't made any promises of salvation on those acts. Baptism in the New Testament was a full immersion in water, and since that's what God attached His promises to, that's how we should teach it today also.

The Church of Christ

How we teach salvation is a big deal! After all, salvation is at the heart of the gospel. Jesus came to "seek and to save the lost" (Luke 19:10), and His gospel is the "power of God for salvation" (Romans 1:16). God wants us to be saved through Christ; that's why Jesus died on the cross for our sins. And God has given us His terms for uniting our souls with the saving death of Christ, so we must honor those commands and promises of God over the opinions of man.

Our religious world desperately needs to restore God's teaching on how to be saved. I suppose we could just tell everyone that it didn't matter, and that no matter how they try to become a Christian that they will be okay eternally. If we did that, I'm sure some people today would praise us for being "loving" people, and they would consider us to be "non-judgmental." But no matter what people thought about it, there's a big problem with telling people that how you become a Christian doesn't matter: we are not God, and so we don't get to hand out tickets to heaven. All people would get is a human promise from us – and human promises can be wrong. So we need to be careful about telling people that we know they are saved if they haven't obeyed the gospel in the way God taught. We don't get to make that decision.

In the churches of Christ, we are trying to teach salvation the way God taught it in the Bible. Hear, Believe, Repent, Confess, and be Baptized is a good summary of the New Testament teaching. When we've done those things, we know we have the promises of God. We gladly trust God to be the final judge of those who are taught salvation differently from what His word says, but we also must recognize that God has not made any promises about salvation besides the way He shows us in the New Testament. So if we meet someone who has been taught a different way to be saved, we try to sit down with them and show them – in a sincere spirit of love – what the Bible says about how to receive salvation in Christ. And we encourage them to do it God's way. Have you done it God's way? If not, receive salvation God's way, and then you can rejoice in the confidence of having the promises of God.

The "Seed Principle"

And here's another great thing about becoming a Christian God's way: when you simply follow God's teachings on how to be saved, do you know what it makes you? It makes you a Christian. Nothing more, nothing less. Not a member of a denomination. Not a follower of a particular preacher. Not a part of a man-made church or teaching. Following only God's word on how to be saved through Christ makes you a Christian only.

I've heard preachers talk about the "seed principle," from one of Jesus' parables in which He compared the word of

God to a seed (Luke 8:11). When you plant a tomato seed, guess what comes up? A tomato. If you plant a watermelon seed, guess what comes up? You guessed it, a watermelon. If someone claims they planted tomato seeds, and then squash plants grew up, you know they either lied or made a mistake. You would never believe that actual tomato seeds produce anything other than tomatoes, and you'd be right. Whatever seed you plant is the one that grows.

Well, the preachers sometimes say, what seed will I plant in trying to receive salvation through Christ? If I plant the denominational creed book's teaching, then it produces members of that denomination. If I plant whatever the preacher's opinion is, then it produces followers of that preacher's opinion. If I plant human tradition, I get followers of human tradition. But if I simply plant the word of God, and what it teaches on salvation, then what I get is a Christian. I just want to be a Christian. Don't you? Let's help others see what God's word teaches on salvation, so that they can rejoice in the promises of God (not the promises of people) as Christians, and Christians only.

Discussion Questions

1) How would you summarize the Bible's teaching on how to be saved? What verses stand out to you?
2) Why do people teach the idea of "faith only?" What verses in the Bible show some problems with teaching "faith only?"
3) How can we encourage people to see that both faith and baptism must go together?
4) Why do you think people baptize babies? What does the Bible say about children and salvation?

5) Many people in our religious world seem to think baptism is not important. What makes you think baptism is important from the life and teaching of Jesus? (Read Matthew 3:13-17, Matthew 28:18-20, and John 3:1-5 for some starting points.) What makes you think it's important from the Book of Acts? (Hint: look at how people became Christians in Acts.)
6) What are some of the promises God makes about baptism when it is united with faith? Make a list of verses about baptism, and write beside it what each verse promises in baptism.
7) Do you think it's wise to take only a few verses on a biblical topic and emphasize them while neglecting other verses on that topic? How does that apply to the study of biblical topics like salvation?
8) What are the dangers of telling people that we know they are saved if they haven't become a Christian God's way?
9) What did this chapter mean by the "seed principle," and how does it apply to pursuing undenominational Christianity?

Personal Reflection

1) If you have made the effort to try to become a Christian, how did you do it? Was it the same or different from how we've seen in this chapter? Who taught you and how?
2) If someone asked you how to become a Christian, could you show them from the Bible? Perhaps we need to memorize some of the passages in this chapter, or write them in our Bible somewhere where we

can easily get to them. Let's be ready to share "how to become a Christian" whenever God opens a door for that conversation.

3) When we have become a Christian God's way, we have the promises of God on salvation! Why should that be comforting to us? Look at Titus 1:2 and Hebrews 6:18 and what they say about God and His promises.

CHAPTER 7

Restoring God's Plan For Church Leadership

"When they had appointed elders for them in every church,
having prayed with fasting, they commended them
to the Lord in whom they had believed."
- Acts 14:23

Starters

- Make a list of different church leadership positions and titles you see around the religious world. (Examples: pastor, priest, etc.)
- Do you think it matters how we organize church leadership? Why or why not?
- If you currently go to a church, who are the people who have "official" leadership positions in the congregation? What are their roles? How did they come to be in those positions?

Who's In Charge?

We have been looking around our religious world and noticing all the differences in teachings and practices. And we are trying to have the wisdom not only to notice those differences, but also to dig through the clutter to see what God wants His church to be. We have seen that we need to restore Scripture to its proper place of authority, to stop giving authority to all the manmade handbooks and creeds and councils. We then saw that we need to go back to teaching "how to be saved" the way it was taught in the New Testament, rejecting some of the manmade promises and half-teachings that are given today about salvation. I suppose our list of religious differences could become a long list, but we are trying to at least discuss some big first steps that are needed to restore God's plan for His church back toward what He wanted it to be.

Another way our religious world has really messed up God's plan for His church is in church leadership. Different groups all seem to have different forms of church leadership. There are pastors. There are preachers. There are bishops. There are priests and deacons and cardinals. Some call themselves apostles, and some are declared popes. Some are voted as denominational presidents. Some want to be called "father" or "reverend." You can probably name many other religious titles. All these different positions, and all claiming leadership in Christ's church. Are any of these what God wanted His church leadership to look like? Did God have a way He wanted church leadership to function?

God's Chosen Leaders

How should we decide the way to organize church leadership? Let's start simple with a few reminders. Jesus Christ is the head of His church, as we see in Ephesians 1:22-23 and Colossians 1:18. Jesus built His church (Matthew 16:18) and bought it with His own blood (Acts 20:28). So Jesus gets to decide who leads His church. We must constantly be reminded that men don't get to make decisions for Jesus and His church! And as we've seen, Jesus gave His inspired word to the apostles, who recorded it in Scripture. So if we want to know how God wants his church to be led, where do we look? Not in a creed or handbook or in religious tradition or religious history. We must let Scripture decide the matter; that's where God has spoken clearly about what He wants in His church.

So what does God say in Scripture? As we read through the New Testament, we find that Jesus did in fact give His plan for church leadership. Jesus initially chose apostles, who would become the teachers and leaders in the establishment of the church. The apostles would then hand church leadership to men with certain qualifications, in a role the Bible usually calls "elders" (they are also sometimes called shepherds or overseers). Each individual congregation would thereafter be led by elders, who would have responsibility for spiritual leadership, but under the higher authority of Christ and His word. Let's lay out how that happens in the New Testament.

Church Leadership Started With the Apostles

Here are a few broad brushstrokes on the role of the apostles in the New Testament:

- **Chosen to learn from Jesus**. Jesus chose 12 men from among His many disciples to serve in the special role of apostles (Matthew 10:1-4). They would learn from Jesus, and would also help Jesus share His message with others.

- **Promised to receive the inspiration of the Holy Spirit.** Before He died, Jesus told the apostles that when He ascended back to heaven, He would send them the Holy Spirit in a special way. The Holy Spirit would speak through the apostles in teaching the world about Jesus and what He wanted in His people (John 14:16-17,26; John 15:26-27, John 16:13-15).
- **Mission to take the gospel to the world**. After He rose from the dead, Jesus told the apostles that they would soon receive the Holy Spirit's power and then take the gospel to all nations (Acts 1:4-8).
- **Their teaching would set the pattern for the church**. As Christianity spread around the world, the apostles' inspired teaching was to be the foundation of the church (Ephesians 2:19-20).
- **The first church leaders**. The apostles were the first church leaders in Jerusalem, where the church began before the gospel spread throughout the world. In addition to teaching, the apostles made decisions about what to do with money that was given to God's work (Acts 4:36-37, 5:1-2) and how to handle church problems and ministries (Acts 6:1-4).
- **The apostles' role would not last forever**. Paul wrote that Jesus appeared to him and called him to be an apostle "last of all" (1 Corinthians 15:7-8). Paul called it his "untimely" beginning as an apostle, since he was called last and long after the other apostles. There would not be any more apostles added after Paul.

Of course, the apostles would not live forever, and the church would spread all over the world, so in the New Testament we see the apostles teaching how the church should be led without the presence of the apostles. We find God's plan for elder-led churches, which we will see next.

The Apostles Handed Church Leadership to Elders

Let's take the same broad-brushstroke approach to see how the apostles handed off the role of church leadership to elders:

- **Elders begin leading in the church.** The first reference to a church leadership beyond the apostles is in Acts 11:30, where a contribution is sent to Jerusalem for the poor Christians, and they give it to "the **elders**." Since Christians used to bring contributions to the apostles in Jerusalem (in Acts 4:37 and Acts 5:2), this shows that elders are now the leaders of the Jerusalem church. The apostles had begun to travel more to preach, so they had handed the leadership role in Jerusalem to elders.
- **Elders appointed in every church**. After Paul and Barnabas went on their first missionary journey, establishing churches in cities around the Roman empire, they went back through those cities and "appointed elders for them in every church" (Acts 14:23).
- **Elders working with the apostles**. The Jerusalem elders worked alongside the apostles in wrestling with the issue of whether Gentiles had to be circumcised and follow the Old Testament Law of Moses (Acts 15:2). This shows us the apostles' respect for the elders' role as church leaders, as well as the apostles' desire to help the elders grow in their leadership. (By the way, since the apostles were inspired by the Holy Spirit in a special way, this

group in Acts 15 sent a letter to the churches that gave an answer not just from men, but from the Holy Spirit, as we see in Acts 15:22-23,28. The apostles' presence gave this group a unique authority from God that no future man-made "council" could have.)

- **Paul's instructions to elders**. In Acts 20:17-38, Paul meets with the elders of the church at Ephesus. It feels like a good-bye speech, as Paul knows he won't be with them forever, and he encourages them to lead and guard the Ephesian church in the way the Holy Spirit wanted them to. (More on this passage in a minute – it is key for the role of an elder.)
- **Selecting Elders.** Paul would later tell Titus to appoint elders in every city, and he gave qualifications for what these men should be (Titus 1:5-9). He also calls them "*overseers*" (v. 7). Notice that Paul didn't want Titus (a preacher) to be in charge of the church; he wanted Titus to help each church "set in order" the leadership of elders. Paul gives similar instructions to Timothy in 1 Timothy 3:1-7, which also gives qualifications for "overseers." (If a church did not have men who met these qualifications to be elders, we assume they simply did their best to serve God without elders, until the time came when they could appoint qualified men.)
- **Always at least two elders leading a church**. You will also notice in these passages that the New Testament only mentions a church's "elders" as plural – you never see just one elder leading a church by himself in the New Testament; it was always at least two men serving together as "elders" over a church. Apparently God wanted the collective wisdom of two or more godly men to

lead, not just one man, who might have blind spots and limitations, no matter how well-meaning he might be.

- **Peter's instructions to elders**. Peter served as an elder in a church later in his life. Perhaps other apostles did also. (The apostle John calls himself an "elder" in 2nd John 1 and 3rd John 1, which might be a reference to his old age, or it might mean that he was serving as an elder in a church.) Notice what Peter wrote in 1 Peter 5:1-4, which shows us that elders were supposed to do the "shepherding" (sometimes called "pastoring") in each church:

  > *(1) Therefore, I exhort the elders among you, as your fellow elder and witness of the sufferings of Christ, and a partaker also of the glory that is to be revealed, (2) shepherd the flock of God among you, exercising oversight not under compulsion, but voluntarily, according to the will of God; and not for sordid gain, but with eagerness; (3) nor yet as lording it over those allotted to your charge, but proving to be examples to the flock. (4) And when the Chief Shepherd appears, you will receive the unfading crown of glory.*

  That passage shows that God had given elders the "oversight" of the flock. They were supposed to live as good examples, not be oppressive in their leadership, and remember that they themselves served under the authority of the "Chief Shepherd."

Elders, Deacons, and Preachers: How They Fit Together

Deacons and Preachers are also mentioned in the New Testament. What were their roles?

- **What about deacons**? After giving qualifications for overseers, 1 Timothy 3:8-15 goes on to give qualifications for "deacons." The word deacon literally means "servant," so these were special servants in the church. Most people agree that Acts 6:1-7 gives an example for how deacons were to function, as appointed servants put in charge of a ministry by the church leaders. We see Paul write a letter to the church at Philippi, "including the overseers and deacons" (Phil. 1:1). So deacons were not the overseers of the church, but were in the role of special servants under the leadership of the elders.

- **What about preachers**? Preachers (also called ministers or evangelists) such as Timothy and Titus were to preach the word of God (2 Timothy 4:2) and help churches organize according to God's word (Titus 1:5), such as helping churches appoint elders as their spiritual leaders. Preachers are to share the gospel like the apostles did, but preachers do not have church authority like the apostles did. Preachers are not given the role of decision-making for the congregation, and they are not "in charge." The only "authority" preachers have is the authority of the message they preach, the word of God.
- **Understanding these distinct roles**. So after the passing of the apostles, elders – men who must meet God's qualifications – are appointed to have spiritual leadership in each church. Deacons, who also must meet God-given qualifications, are appointed to serve under the elders as leaders of particular ministries. Preachers do not have an authority position, but their role is important: they are to teach God's word and help churches, wherever they go.

What Are Elders Supposed to Do?

So what were the elders supposed to do to provide spiritual leadership in the churches? One of the best passages to study the role of elders is Acts chapter 20, where Paul is instructing the Ephesian elders in what God wants them to do. The entire section of Acts 20:17-38 is worth reading, but we want to notice especially verses 28-32, where Paul focuses on what the elders were supposed to be doing:

> *(28) Be on guard for yourselves and for all the flock, among which the Holy Spirit has made you overseers, to shepherd the church of God which He purchased with His own blood. (29) I know that after my departure savage wolves will come in among you, not sparing the flock; (30) and from among your own selves men will arise, speaking perverse things, to draw away the disciples after them. (31) Therefore be on the alert, remembering that night and day for a period of three years I did not cease to admonish each one with tears. (32) And now I commend you to God and to the word of His grace, which is able to build you up and to give you the inheritance among all those who are sanctified.*

Just like in 1 Peter 5:1-4 earlier, here we see the role of elder described as a shepherding role. In understanding what elders should be doing, many find it helpful to explore what actual shepherds do for their flocks, and then notice how "spiritual shepherds" do the same thing in leading the congregation. Here are some brief thoughts on it.

What are elders supposed to do to "shepherd the church of God?"

- **Shepherds feed and water the flock**. Just as shepherds help the sheep find the food and water that gives them life and strength, elders must help the church have the spiritual needs that build spiritual life and strength. That means making sure the church has spiritual growth opportunities such as Bible-teaching, worship, service, and fellowship. Part of an elder's qualifications is the ability to teach God's word (1 Tim. 3:2, Titus 1:9). The elders are not the only ones who teach (remember, for example, preachers also are to preach the word, 2 Timothy 4:2), but elders participate in church teaching in various ways, and they make sure the congregation has plenty of biblical teaching and biblical practice to nourish the faith of the church.

- **Shepherds protect the flock**. As Paul says in Acts 20:29-31, protecting the flock includes keeping false teachings and false teachers from harming the church. It also includes seeking out members of the flock when they are in danger of becoming spiritually sick or lost, and trying to bring them back into the fold of Christ. Elders will occasionally have serious conversations with those who are getting tangled in sin, and in certain circumstances they may even need to protect the church from sin by withdrawing fellowship from someone who refuses to give up a sinful lifestyle (Matthew 18:15-17, 1 Corinthians 5).
- **Shepherds know the flock.** In John 10:4-5, Jesus says that He (as the Good Shepherd) and His sheep know each other. Shepherds spend time with the flock, on good days and bad days. They watch the sheep grow and change. To best lead spiritually, elders must strive to have relationships and understanding of their congregation and their context. Like so many things, relationships are important! You cannot effectively shepherd from

afar, which is perhaps another reason God wanted each church to have its own eldership.

- **Shepherds are in charge of the flock.** Paul says that God made these men "overseers" in verse 28. Shepherds are in charge of the flock, and must decide which direction the flock should go. In some ways, all Christians "shepherd" each other through encouragement, but only the elders have the shepherd's *oversight role* of the flock. God gives elders the responsibility of leading and making spiritual decisions for the church, sometimes in difficult circumstances. They must make these decisions according to "God and the word of His grace" (Acts 20:32), and not according to popularity or culture or any other standard.
- **Shepherds must also "guard themselves" (Acts 20:28).** If the shepherd is defeated by an enemy, he can't lead the flock anymore! God gave spiritual qualifications for elders because He wants a certain type of spiritual leader. God didn't mention anything about income level or earthly success when He gave the qualifications for elders in 1 Timothy 3 and Titus 1. God wanted certain spiritual qualities, men of strong faith. Elders must make sure that they continue to grow in their own faith, so that they can be the spiritual examples and leaders that God desires.

Clearly, elders have an important role in God's church! Acts 20:28 says when elders are chosen to lead according to God's qualifications, it is the "Holy Spirit" that actually makes them overseers, because the Holy Spirit gave the qualifications. So these men are in a special role, as God's chosen leaders for His church. They are the ones to whom God gave the shepherding and oversight role. God expects them to guard and direct His church in faithful Christian living as best they can.

Where We Need to Fix It

I think the biblical pattern is clear: the inspired apostles taught that after they passed on, elders were supposed to continue as the leaders in each local congregation. This was God's plan. In the Bible, you don't see the complicated denominational structures we have built up today. Sadly, God's plan is rarely seen today. What do we need to do to try to fix it?

1) **We need to get rid of the man-made leadership structures in the denominational world.** Perhaps the Catholic church is the best-known example of a man-made leadership hierarchy that is different from the plan of God we see in the New Testament. That is not to say anything unkind about Catholics; many of us have friends and family of Catholic backgrounds who we love and appreciate. But the Catholic leadership structure was created by men, not by God. God did not want a pope leading every Christian in the world. God did not want cardinals or bishops with authority over many churches. And Catholics are certainly not alone in man-made leadership structures: God did not give us denominational conventions to make rules for a multitude of churches. God did not give us denominational boards or presidents over multiple congregations. Wow, you talk about a major reshaping of our religious world – going back to God's plan would be a big change! But do we have the courage and faith to do it God's way, or do we think our human traditions are better than God's plan?

2) **We need to appoint church leaders with the roles and responsibilities God gave them.** As we get rid of the man-made leadership structures, we need to put God's plan back in place: God wanted a group of elders to lead each congregation. He wanted Scripture to be the standard for the elders to uphold. He wanted deacons to lead ministries under the elders' oversight. He wanted preachers to preach God's word, and to help churches know God's will as found in Scripture. We need to drop our religious leadership traditions, and we need to appoint church leaders with the roles and responsibilities God gave them.

3) **We need to stop confusing "preachers" and "pastors."** Many churches today have given church authority to a preacher, often giving him the title of "pastor." The word "pastor" is one translation of "shepherd." As we have seen, the New Testament gives the description of "shepherd" only to elders, not to preachers. The elders were supposed to meet the list of qualities given in 1 Timothy 3:1-7 and Titus 1:5-9, and there were always at least two or more elders in a congregation, not one man leading everyone else. The one-man "pastor system" of many churches is not what God wanted.

   Preachers will naturally help toward some of the goals of shepherds – teaching, for instance – like every Christian should. But preachers and shepherds are different roles, because shepherds are in charge of the flock, while preachers are supposed to teach God's word. God did not want preachers to take over the decision-making and church discipline responsibilities like they often do today. It was possible in the Bible for a preacher to also serve as one of the elders if he met God's qualifications – like Peter, for example – but if a preacher does not meet God's requirements in 1 Timothy 3:1-7 and Titus 1:5-9, he doesn't need to be an elder, and we don't need to be calling him a "pastor." Preachers need to be serving as preachers, and elders need to be serving as elders, trusting God's plan for church leadership.

Does Church Leadership Matter?

Is church leadership really that big of a deal? That all depends on how much you trust God and His plan for His church. When God had the apostles hand leadership responsibilities to elders, did God know what He was doing? Do we think that man was able to somehow improve on God's plan by making our own hierarchies? After all, you remember, Christians are supposed to continue in the traditions given by the apostles (2 Thess. 2:15, Phil. 4:9, Jude 3)!

I imagine that when men started creating their own church leadership structures, they probably thought they were helping God. Perhaps they thought that having one man leading multiple churches would help keep all those churches in line with God's word. And if that was so good, then maybe having one man over a larger number of churches would help even more churches stay in line. Soon, making a religious hierarchy may have sounded pretty good. Perhaps they never considered the possibility that one man leading many churches could have the opposite effect also: if he becomes unfaithful to God's plan, his authority leads all the churches in the wrong direction. No matter what the motives are for designing a different leadership structure, it's not wise – and it's not right – to try to change God's plan.

I think God knows what He's doing; He doesn't need us to "improve" His plan for church leadership. We've obviously tried that, and it has led us to the problematic, unbiblical systems of religious authority that we have today. Our additions end up blocking people's view of how the church is supposed to function. Let's go back to God's plan, and trust that He knows what's best for His church.

The Church of Christ

In trying to simply be the church of Christ as found in the Bible, you will find that churches of Christ have organized our religious leadership the way it is described in the New Testament. The apostles' time has passed, so elders are appointed to lead each congregation, and those elders must answer to the authority of Christ and His word. They are chosen according to God's qualifications in 1 Timothy 3:1-7 and Titus 1:5-9. They are given the responsibilities of spiritual shepherds, as God described their role (Acts 20:28-32, 1 Peter 5:1-4).

Under the oversight of the elders, deacons are appointed to lead various church ministries. These men are chosen according to the qualifications given in 1 Timothy 3:8-15.

We also have preachers, whose role is to preach Scripture and encourage people to follow it. They do not have oversight authority of a church. They help churches by serving in a teaching and evangelizing role (2 Timothy 4:2,5), and they are expected to live what they teach, as strong examples of Christian living (1 Timothy 4:12).

We have no other religious hierarchy. No pope or church president or denominational headquarters or councils or conventions or anything like that. If God wanted those structures for leading His church, He would have asked for it. We are trying to trust and follow God's plan for His church. We would love for you to join us in that goal.

What's Next...

In Chapter 8, we will discuss one more area that we believe is in need of restoration in today's religious world: church worship. It's another topic on which our world is tempted to think we can improve on what God wanted, and we end up forgetting what worship is intended for. What did God want from worship? Let's explore it together in the next chapter.

Discussion Questions

1) What was unique about the role of the 12 apostles? Who does the Bible say was the last one called to the role of an apostle (1 Cor. 15:8-9)?
2) How does the description of elders as "shepherds" (Acts 20:28) help us understand their role? How do they carry out that role?
3) Should every Christian be part of helping "shepherd" each other in some ways? How? Yet God only gives the title of shepherd to elders. So how is the elders' shepherding role different from the ways in which we all care for each other? (Hint: the next question may help.)
4) There is an "oversight" role for elders (they are often called "overseers"). Give some examples of the types of things elders must decide for a church family. Which responsibilities do you think would be the most difficult?

5) Can elders just do whatever they want, since they have authority in the church? Who or what has authority over them?
6) Read through 1 Timothy 3:1-7 and Titus 1:5-9. Why do you think God gave these specific qualifications for church leaders? Why didn't He mention anything about wealth or status or power?
7) 1 Peter 5:3 says that elders should not "lord over" the flock. What does that mean? Read Matthew 20:25-28. If church leaders are truly following the attitude of Jesus, how will that affect the way they lead the church?
8) How are the "hierarchy system" and the "pastor system" different from God's plan for church leadership?
9) Read 1 Timothy 3:1 and 3:13. What do those verses tell us about how God feels about those who are willing to lead and serve in His church?
10) Why do you think it matters that we organize church leadership the way they did in the New Testament?

Personal Reflection

1) Read Hebrews 13:17. What can you do to help elders lead the church "with joy and not with grief?" If you have elders in the church you worship with, what could you do this week to encourage them?
2) If you were part of a church that didn't have biblical leadership the way God wanted it, what would you do? What do you think God would want you to do?
3) If your life circumstances don't match the qualifications for an elder or deacon, does that mean there is

no role for you in God's church? How can you be a leader among God's people even if you are not in an official leadership role? (Hint: read Matthew 5:16 and Romans 12:4-8 for good places to start.) God's church needs all of us!

CHAPTER 8

Restoring God's Plan For Worship

"For an hour is coming, and now is, when the true worshipers will worship the Father in spirit and truth; for such people the Father seeks to be His worshipers."
-Jesus, in John 4:23

Starters

- Name some different ways churches worship God in today's religious world. How do you think churches decide the ways they will worship?
- Do you think it matters how we worship God? Why or why not?
- Why do you think God wants us to worship Him at all? What does He hope it will produce in us?
- How does your church worship God? How did they decide what they would and wouldn't do?

Does How We Worship Matter?

We find something surprising in the Bible's first mention of worship. It comes in Genesis chapter 4, after Adam and Eve have sinned and been put out of the Garden of Eden. Some time has passed, and two of their sons, Cain and Abel, each bring an offering to God. We might assume that their family has already been offering worship to God for many years, but this is the first time the Bible has told us about it. Cain "brought an offering to the Lord of the fruit of the ground," (v. 3), while Abel "on his part also brought of the firstlings of his flock and of their fat portions" (v. 4). What we find next is something that our religious world doesn't usually think is possible: "And the Lord had regard for Abel and for his offering; but for Cain and for his offering He had no regard" (v. 4-5).

What? You mean God accepted Abel's worship and didn't accept Cain's? Why? Well, the text doesn't say. Maybe it's because Abel brought "firstlings," perhaps hinting that Cain brought leftovers instead of his best crops. Maybe Abel's heart was right and Cain's wasn't. Maybe God had asked for an animal sacrifice and Cain brought a crops sacrifice instead. Whatever the reason, Hebrews 11:4 simply says that Abel showed his faith by giving God a better sacrifice.

But let's not get too sidetracked and miss a larger point. It's the very first mention of worship in the Bible, and God gives us an important teaching on worship, one that will run throughout Scripture: *God doesn't accept all worship.* We see it for example when Jesus was speaking to the woman at the well in John 4:23-24, where He talked about "true worshipers." If there are "true worshipers," then it must also be possible to be a "false worshiper." Jesus went on to say that God "seeks" true worshipers who worship Him in spirit and in truth. God desires true worship, and He rejects false worship.

Why would God not accept just any worship? Some people today seem to think this is unfair, as if God should be happy with anything we might give Him in worship. What they're missing is that the one true God really is worthy of worship that honors Him. After all, worship is supposed to be *for* Him! Let's look at some ways that modern-day churches – if we want to be pleasing to God – need to get back to worship as God intended, so we can be the true worshipers God wants us to be.

Restoring the Focus of Christian Worship

When we understand what worship is, we quickly realize that only God is worthy of worship. We "worship" when we offer an act of spiritual adoration, praise, and reverence, to one we consider greater and higher than us. As Christians, we do lots of things "for" God (helping others, for example), but worship is when we bring something as a spiritual offering of praise "to" God. God is the only truly-worthy recipient of worship. It is not right to worship ourselves. It is not right to worship idols (Exod. 20:4-5). It is not right to worship people (Acts 10:25-26). In Revelation 19.9-10, John falls down to worship an angel, and the angel tells John not to worship him, an angel who is merely a fellow servant, but instead to "worship God."

Since God alone is worthy of worship, He alone decides what worship is worthy. That's the first, so-simple-we-sometimes-forget-it thing to remember about worship: worship is supposed to be about God. It is for Him. If it does not please God, our worship is a failure.

We have been looking around our religious world over the last few chapters and noticing the many differences. And worship is definitely another area where there are lots of differences! If we're paying attention, we quickly notice that modern-day worship decisions don't always seem to be focused on what God wants. Sadly, many churches make their worship decisions based on what people like. What will help us get the most people in the door? Do people want "worship" to be a rock concert atmosphere? OK, we will give it to them! Do people want flashing theater lights and a Broadway-style performance? OK, let's do it! Do people like preaching from the Bible or would they rather have life-success presentations? Or just story-telling time? Let's find out and give the people what they want!

All of this seems so backwards. The church is not in the entertainment business; at least it's not supposed to be. If we start making worship decisions based first on what people want, we have lost the focus of Christian worship. Worship, first and last, is about God and what He wants. The only audience in worship is God. People are not the audience, we are supposed to be the worshipers. Yet we often act as if we are trying to "draw an audience" by worshiping with whatever we think people will like. Perhaps we think that we can improve on God's way of worship, that if He would just let us do it our way, we could really change the world for Him. But I trust God knows what worship should be more than we do, and you don't see anywhere in Scripture where God said, "Worship in whatever ways your community likes so that more people will come and your church can be bigger." The standard of worship is not what people like. The standard of worship is whether God is pleased with it. If people think it's fun and exciting, but God is not pleased, we have failed, no matter the worldly applause or the size of the "audience." That doesn't mean that worship should be unmeaningful, it simply means that worship should be about God, not about me. (In fact, if our worship is truly focused on God, it will be meaningful and it will build us up spiritually.)

How Do We Know If God Is Pleased?

When we restore the right focus of Christian worship – a focus on what God wants – we can begin asking the right questions about worship. Before we ask anything about our preferences, our first question should always be: will God be pleased with this offering of worship or not? God has given us several reasons why He may not accept our worship, and we need to know them to make sure our focus stays in the right place. Here are some of the biblical reasons God may be displeased with worship:

1) **God does not accept Performance Worship**. Read Matthew chapter 6, verses 1 and 5, and notice Jesus teaching that God has no reward for worship that is designed to be a performance for other people. Worship is not for a preacher to put on a "performance." Worship is not for people to show off their talents. Worship is not a production. Worship is not treating an audience to a theme-park style "experience." Since Jesus says performance worship has no reward from God, true worshipers will not seek to honor themselves with their "great performance." True worshipers bring a desire to honor God alone.
2) **God does not accept Hypocritical Worship.** Read Matthew 5:23-24 and see Jesus saying that if we have sinned against someone, we need to try to make things right with them first and then come to worship God.

Read Amos 5:21-24, and see that God hated the Israelites' worship because their lives were not showing "justice" or "righteousness" (v. 24). False worshipers aren't trying to live for God, but they hope that an occasional worship service will cover over their sinful lifestyles. True worshipers bring to God a life that genuinely wants to live for Him.

3) **God does not accept Heartless Worship.** Read Malachi 1:6-14 and see God's frustration when the Israelites gave God their leftovers and second-best in worship. God is dishonored when we give people in our life more respect than we give God in our worship (v. 8). God is dishonored when we complain at how tiresome it is to take time to worship Him (v. 13). They weren't putting any spiritual effort into making their worship meaningful, and so God wished someone would just shut the gates (v. 10) instead of dishonoring Him with empty worship acts. As Jesus said, we should truly worship God "in spirit" (John 4:23-24), not just going through the motions. True worshipers bring a heart that is truly giving praise and desiring to grow closer to God.

4) **God does not accept Uncommanded Worship.** Read Leviticus 10:1-3 and see the serious message God gave the Israelites about worshiping Him in ways that He had not commanded or asked for. The problem: Nadab and Abihu "offered strange fire before the Lord, which He had not commanded them" (v. 2). False worship seeks to give God whatever form of worship *we* want to give. True worshipers listen to God's word and give God the forms of worship He has asked for.

5) **God does not accept Irreverent Worship.** Read 1 Corinthians 14:26-40 and see Paul teaching the Corinthian

church to worship God in a rational, reverent, orderly manner. They had the miraculous gifts of the Holy Spirit in the days of the apostles, and the Corinthians were using them improperly in their worship. Their worship assemblies had become chaotic and self-serving, and they dishonored God by making His church appear to be out of control (v. 23) instead of truly pointing people toward God. Paul tells them that "God is not a God of confusion but of peace," and that God does not promote chaos in His people (v. 33). Paul ends this section saying that "all things must be done properly and in an orderly manner" (v. 40). That doesn't mean that worship should be stale or overly formal to the point that it lacks feeling; but it means that we should show self-control in honoring God with reverence alongside our heart-felt emotion. Christian worship services are not to be sports cheering sections or rock concerts or school pep rallies, where volume and chaos are the measures of whether a crowd is really "into it." Instead, our emotions should be channeled in worship toward the God who deserves "acceptable service with reverence and awe" (Heb. 12:28). Christian worship assemblies are supposed to be both meaningful and reverent at the same time, worshiping the Almighty King with both our spirits and our minds (1 Cor. 14:15).

I'm well aware that listing these types of worship that God rejects is not exactly a popular thing to say or study today. But they are in the Bible, so if we're serious about wanting to please God (as we should be), I don't think we can ignore God's teaching on true worship, even if everyone else seems to think that how we worship doesn't matter. If we're truly trying to be a church that follows God, and not just trying to play church or see how popular we can make our churches, we must turn our worship focus back towards God. God is the standard of worship, and we need to make sure we are worshiping Him in the ways that honor Him. That means evaluating our worship goals to make sure we aren't encouraging Performance Worship, or Hypocritical Worship, or Heartless Worship, or Uncommanded Worship, or Irreverent Worship.

Restoring the Acts of Christian Worship

So if you and I are just trying to be Christians, and just trying to please God with our worship, how will we decide what to do in our worship assemblies? We wouldn't take a poll to find what people like, nor would we study the latest trends in religion. We're trying to please God, and so we look in God's word to see what God wants in worship. That only makes sense, doesn't it, if worship is for Him?

As Christians, we are under the covenant of Christ (Heb. 9:15), so we look in the New Testament to see what forms of worship God requested from His church. As you read through your New Testament, I think you will find five worship acts, all five of which the church in the Bible offered to God as worship:

1) **Prayer** – Acts 4:23-31, 1 Timothy 2:1-2.
2) **Singing** – Ephesians 5:19, Colossians 3:16, 1 Corinthians 14:15, Matthew 26:30, Acts 16:25.
3) **Scripture Reading and Preaching** – Acts 20:7, 1 Timothy 4:13.
4) **Giving** to support ministries of the church – 1 Corinthians 16:1-2, 2 Corinthians 9:7.
5) Taking the **Lord's Supper** together each Sunday – Acts 20:7, 1 Corinthians 11:17-34, Acts 2:42.

These are the five things you find Christians doing in the New Testament as worship to God. They worshiped in all five ways on the first day of each week in their church assemblies. They also worshiped in the first four acts (prayer, singing, Scripture, and giving) privately as individuals or in smaller group settings throughout the week.

If you and I are trying to be a church that pleases God with our worship, do you think we should start adding other forms of worship to those? Why would we? As we have seen in the Bible, God has rejected worship that He did not ask for (Lev. 10:1-3). We have also seen that we are supposed to follow the Christian traditions given by the apostles (1 Cor. 11:2, 2 Thess. 2:15, 2 Tim. 3:14, Jude 3). In the two thousand years since the apostles, men have added several forms of worship that weren't there in the New Testament. But if those things aren't in the commands and church examples of the New Testament, then God hasn't asked for them in worship. So if I'm adding them, I'm not adding them because God asked for them. I must be adding them because people decided they liked them. Is that a good reason to add new forms to Christian worship?

I once heard a preacher describe it like a husband getting Christmas gifts for his wife. His wife had given him a list of things she would like: a new book she is excited to read, or a romantic-comedy movie she really likes, or some shoes they saw in the store. On Christmas morning, the husband watches eagerly as his wife begins to unwrap her gifts. She unwraps the boxes, only to find a men's basketball jersey of her husband's favorite player, a sports book about her husband's favorite team, and some new men's running shoes in her husband's size. She gives her husband a confused look. She finally says, "Honey, I appreciate you wanting to give me some Christmas presents; but these gifts aren't really for me, they're for you." "But dear," the husband replies, "I couldn't give you that other stuff with a heart that was really into it, and you don't want me to give you something half-heartedly do you? So I gave you something I could really be excited about."

Do you think that conversation would go well for him? Why not? Because if you are giving a gift to someone you really care about, you make an effort to give a gift they will be happy with. That's the first priority. And your heart will be full just by knowing you gave a gift that pleased them, and by knowing that the gift-giving will deepen your relationship. If we love God, why would we bring Him a worship 'gift' that is really for us more than Him? We know from the New Testament what God has asked for in worship: Prayer, Singing, Bible reading and preaching, Giving, and the Lord's Supper on the first day of each week. Why would we give Him something different, unless we were making it about us more than about Him?

One Example of Giving God What He Has Asked For: Singing in Worship

Let's give one example of how restoring God's requested acts of worship can be countercultural, and thus requires some thought and perhaps some courage to be different. In churches of Christ we follow the New Testament example of simply singing without instruments in our worship. So when people from different religious backgrounds come to assemblies of the churches of Christ, the lack of musical instruments is one of the first things they notice. No pianos or organs or guitars. Since so much of the religious world uses musical instruments in worshiping God, they understandably ask why we don't. We do our best to explain our commitment to New Testament worship and our desire to give God what He has asked for rather than what we might want. Much of our religious world has never studied this issue, so many of our visitors have no idea that the New Testament church simply sang without instruments in their worship.

As you study this issue, I believe you will find that while God's people used instruments in Old Testament worship (along with animal sacrifices and special feast days, etc.), the New Testament church simply sang in their worship. Every time you find commands or examples of music in Christian worship in the New Testament, it only mentions singing. Here are the passages to read for yourself: Matthew 26:30, Mark 14:26, Acts 16:25, 1 Corinthians 14:15, Ephesians 5:19, Colossians 3:16, Hebrews 2:12, Hebrews 13:15, James 5:13. So in the Bible, followers of Christ simply sang in worship, without instruments. In fact, historically, instruments don't appear in Christian worship at all until they were added by men hundreds of years after the time of the apostles. And you may not know that the word 'acapella,' meaning "without instrumental accompaniment," is Latin for "in the manner of the chapel," providing still further evidence that "voices only" singing was how Christian worship was offered to God (in those Christian "chapels") for centuries.

What does all that tell us? The church of the Bible simply sang in worship to God, as they were taught by the inspired apostles, and this tradition continued for a long time. We believe it was a tradition that God wanted to continue, like the other traditions taught by the apostles. So we are trying to get back to God's plan, and therefore we simply sing in our worship. And it always makes me smile when one of our visitors comments on how encouraging it is to hear the beauty of acapella voices blending together, or how much easier it is to focus on the words of our songs without the distraction of instruments. The New Testament doesn't tell us why God wanted Christians to sing without instruments, but it makes sense to me that God has given us the best way to worship Him, so that's what we try to do.

So I hope the larger point makes sense: if I'm adding a new act of worship that isn't in the New Testament, I must be doing it for myself instead of for God, because God certainly hasn't asked for it. So here's what I would be saying: "I don't know if God wants this, but I want it, so let's do it!" I could never say that in good conscience, if my worship is truly God-centered. God has shown us in the New Testament what He wants in worship: Prayer, Singing, Bible teaching, Giving, and the Lord's Supper on the first day of each week. Out of our love and respect for God, we want to offer Him what He wants in worship, so we follow the worship traditions of the apostles, and we don't add new acts of worship to what He has requested in the New Testament.

The Life-Shaping Role of Worship

I've always loved Exodus 34:29, where Moses is coming down from Mount Sinai after receiving the tablets from God: "It came about when Moses was coming down from Mount Sinai..., that Moses did not know that the skin of his face shone because of his speaking with Him." Moses had spent time with God on Mount Sinai, and as a result Moses was different when he came down the mountain. Moses didn't even realize his face was shining with the glory of God – but everyone else noticed. There is a transformative element to spending time with God in worship, a transformation that we don't always immediately notice in ourselves, but one that is very real.

That's one last reason why worship is important enough to restore back to God's plan. Not only does our worship best honor God when we focus it on Him, and best please God when we worship Him in the ways He has asked for, but also: *how we worship shapes our lives*. No, our faces don't shine like Moses' did, but our lives shine brighter as those who have drawn closer to God. When I come before God in worship with a God-centered focus, it naturally shapes a life that is God-centered. When I make my worship about what God wants and not just about what I want, it builds a godly humility that seeks God's will in my life as well. When I choose to worship God His way rather than doing whatever the world desires, it helps me remember that my life is also about pleasing God, and trusting His way is the best way. God-centered worship best shapes a God-centered life.

But the flip side of that is obvious, too, isn't it? When I make my worship about me and what I want, I am building a selfish, me-centered spirit in my life. When I make my worship about what people want and what might bring the world's applause and approval, I am building a people-pleasing spirit instead of a God-pleasing one. When I make my worship about my performance or someone else's performance, I am building a self-glorifying or people-glorifying spirit. Remember what Paul said in 1 Corinthians 11:17? Worshiping in ways that dishonor God makes us "worse!" Our worship shapes us spiritually, for better or for worse.

Worship is done "in spirit" (John 4:23-24), and so it is a soul-building, spirit-building activity. That's one reason God wanted His people to worship Him regularly, including worshiping together every first day of the week. God is not made any better by our worship; instead, we are made better and more like Christ through God-centered, God-pleasing worship. What's more, our worship shows our world, including visitors and our next generation of young people, just how important it is to put God at the center of all we do. What we worship and how we worship is important. Let's get worship back to what God intended it to be, and allow it to shape us into more God-centered lives.

The Church of Christ

In simply striving to be the church of the Bible, churches of Christ worship God through the acts of worship you find in the New Testament. We strive to keep the focus of worship on God and what He wants, not on what we want or what people want. We certainly have choices to make about how we worship – choices of which songs to sing or what to say in our prayers or what Scripture to preach from – but our first question about worship is always whether God will be pleased.

We believe that true God-centered worship should also be meaningful, life-shaping worship. We do not want our worship to be performance-centered or irreverent, but neither do we want it to be unmeaningful or stale or lifeless. Those of us who lead in worship must put forth the effort in preparation and prayer to lead God's people meaningfully, yet not in a performance-worship manner. All of us who gather in assembled worship must bring hearts ready to truly praise God in our spirits, not bringing heartless worship or a spectator mentality.

In short, we try to take it seriously when Jesus says that God seeks true worshipers to worship Him in spirit and in truth. God thinks it is important, and we would love for our entire religious world to join us in trying to restore worship back to what God intended it to be.

What We've Seen So Far...

This concludes our section on "Getting Back to God's Plan for the Church." We have now studied several big steps that we believe our religious world needs to take to get our churches back toward what God intended His undivided, Christ-centered church to be. Here's what I hope we've seen in this book so far:

- *We need to drop our man-made and denominational names.* God's church is supposed to be undivided and unified, and we build fences and divisions whenever we take other names besides the name of Christ (1 Cor. 1:10-13). We are supposed to simply be Christians.
- *We need to pursue a spirit of restoration*, having the courage to evaluate ourselves and to change whenever we see we have departed from God's plan.
- *We need to get the Bible back to the place of final authority that God intended*. We need to get rid of all the human creeds and traditions that people have grown to trust over Scripture.
- *We need to teach "how to be saved" the way they taught it in the New Testament*. Only the promises of God can be trusted when it comes to eternity, so we must teach God's way for receiving salvation in Christ. We saw a good biblical summary of how to become a Christian: hear, believe, repent, confess, and be baptized. We must not teach faith without baptism or baptism without faith, but faith and bap-

tism going hand in hand together with a repentant life.

- *We need to get church leadership roles back to the roles God gave His church*: elders as shepherds who meet God's qualifications to lead their local congregation, deacons who lead ministries under the spiritual authority of the elders, and preachers who preach the gospel without assuming an oversight role that God wanted elders to have. We need to get rid of church hierarchies and denominational structures, instead doing it the New Testament way: each congregation having its own leadership under the authority of Christ and His word.
- *We need to get church worship back to what God wanted it to be*. Worship should be God-focused, not man-focused, and with the acts of worship that God gave His church in the New Testament.

Just imagine if all churches pursued those biblical goals! No denominations. No creed-books. No man-centered worship practices. No more man-made or half-biblical promises of salvation. Instead, churches trying to follow God's word alone, teaching, leading, and worshiping in the ways God gave His church! The church would be a lot more of what God wanted it to be, and I think we would all discover that God's way really is best. Just think of what God could do through us if we all trusted Him enough to do things His way!

What's Next...

In the next couple of chapters, we will try to complete the big picture of what God wants His church to be. God's goals for His church are even bigger than just trying to get the issues right (although trying to get the issues right is important). As we will see, the church should operate in three directions, and if we want to please God, we need to pursue all three directions as best we can. Sometimes, amidst all the clutter of different ideas, we can forget about God's "big picture goals" for His people. What does God want us to be doing as a church? Let's put a couple more pieces together in the next two chapters...

Discussion Questions

1) Why do you think so many people believe God will accept all worship no matter what?
2) Read 1 Corinthians 11:17. How could worship assemblies make us "worse" spiritually?
3) How might churches put people-pleasing above God-pleasing in their worship?
4) Do you think our entertainment-oriented culture affects us in how we approach worship? Do you think it makes it easy to fall into a "spectator mentality" or a "performance worship mentality" in our church worship assemblies? How can we work to avoid those problems?
5) Read Hebrews 12:28-29. What are some qualities of God we should remember when we come before Him in worship? What are some ways we can show a lack of reverence in worship?
6) How can we make sure our worship is both meaningful and reverent at the same time? Is it possible for our worship to become stale and lifeless? What responsibility do the worship leaders have to keep this

from happening? What responsibility do the worshipers have?

7) Notice in 1 Corinthians 14:23-25 that Paul wanted the church to be conscious of the message its worship sent to visitors. How can we make sure our worship is understandable to visitors? But another side to consider as well: is it possible to go too far and make worship more about visitors than about God?

8) Why do you think God wanted the church to worship together weekly? How is worship together different from just worshiping alone?

9) Do you believe that how we worship affects how we live? How will God-centered worship affect our spiritual lives differently than self-centered worship?

Personal Reflection

1) Sometimes people confuse "worshiping God" and "glorifying God." While all of our life should "glorify" God (Matthew 5:16), worship is a spiritual act intentionally offered *to* God. For example, in Genesis 22:5, Abraham says that he and Isaac would go over "and worship" and then return. Also, in Acts 8:27, the Ethiopian had gone to Jerusalem "to worship." Notice that worship is a specific act, not every single part of our life. As this chapter described it, we do lots of things "for" God, but worship is when we bring something "to" God.

   So worshiping God and glorifying God are different, yet they are connected. How does your worship to God help your life to glorify God? How does glorifying God with your life make your times of worship more meaningful? How can you use your God-given talents to glorify God in your life?

2) Have I truly been bringing my heart in worship? Read Malachi 1:6-14 and reflect on whether you have allowed worship to become tiresome or without mental effort. Bring God your best heart in worship!

3) Do you have a favorite worship song? Think about the words. How should that song affect your life and your faith?

4) Have you ever studied the issue of whether we should have instrumental music in Christian worship? If you want to dive into it deeper, there are several good sources, including a book called *The Instrumental Music Issue*, by Everett Ferguson, Jack Lewis, and Earl West.

Section 3:
Remembering the Big Picture: Two Other Essential Pieces of God's Plan

CHAPTER 9

God's Plan For Church Relationships

"Bear one another's burdens,
and thereby fulfill the law of Christ."
- Paul, in Galatians 6:2

Starters

- Why do you think Jesus established a church at all? Why not just let everyone live the Christian life on their own?
- If someone who was not a Christian asked you what the church is supposed to do, what would you say?
- What do you think it means in Galatians 6:2 to "bear one another's burdens?"

Church in Three Directions

We have seen that the church is important to God – Christ built it and bought it. We have seen that God had a plan for His church that wasn't supposed to change, which means we must be willing to restore

His plan whenever we have allowed human traditions to mess it up. In the next two chapters, we will explore two other important pieces of God's plan for His church, pieces so essential that no study of the church would be complete without them. Hopefully these studies will help us see the big picture of what God wanted His church to be, and help us recommit ourselves to some goals that churches often struggle to live out.

I have heard it said that the church is supposed to operate in three directions. First, the church operates *upwards*. The church is the community where God is glorified and worshiped. Christians are living out a covenant relationship with God – a relationship established through Jesus Christ – which includes living in ways that honor God and worshiping in ways that honor God. Second, the church operates *inwards*. Christians are supposed to be a support system for their fellow Christians and help each other in faith. Third, the church operates *outwards*. The church is the community that reaches out to the world in the name of Christ, proclaiming the gospel and sharing the love of God to all peoples and nations.

All three directions are important, if the church is to be healthy and doing what God wants it to do. We studied worship (part of the upwards direction) in the last chapter. We will explore outreach (outwards) in the next chapter. In this chapter, let's focus on the church operating inwards, a study that I believe makes it clear why God wanted His people to be together as a "church" in the first place...

Family Was There

I was in second grade when my grandmother on my mom's side passed away. I was too young to really understand all that was going on, but I have a few memories of the days after she passed. I remember my mom crying, and I remember giving her a hug along with my sisters in our living room. But I think more than anything I remember people coming to the house. Family members came from out of town to let my parents know they were hurting with them. Friends from church dropped by, sometimes briefly and sometimes to talk for awhile. I remember being appreciative that people cared enough to come by the house and check on my parents. Looking back, I now realize: that's what family does. Family was hurting, so family was there.

I have noticed similar scenes play out many times in many different circumstances through the years. I'm sure you have too. Someone goes into the hospital, or someone passes away, or someone is going through a difficult time, and suddenly people appear. Family comes in from out of town to check up and see what they can do to help. People call to share a word of encouragement and love. Friends from church drop by to offer a hug and a prayer together. Cards arrive in the mail from others who can't be there in person. That's the way it's supposed to be. When family is hurting, family is there.

In 1 Timothy 3:15, Paul refers to the church as the "household of God." The church is a household – a family! It's the family where God lives and binds each person together. The more I realized that, the more it made sense why friends from church were always present at those family moments of loss or illness. The church is a family. And when family is hurting, family is there.

Bear One Another's Burdens

Paul's words to Christians in Galatians 6:2 are so simple but so important for the church to really be the church: "Bear one another's burdens, and thereby fulfill the law of Christ." What do we learn from that passage?

First, we are reminded that even Christians have "burdens." What? You mean my life won't be pain-free if I give my life to Christ? Despite what you might have heard from some books or televangelists, the Bible never promises a pain-free life. In fact, in Psalm 34:19, the Bible acknowledges, "Many are the afflictions of the righteous." Christians will face sin burdens. They will face health burdens. They will face burdens of life disappointments, broken relationships, financial struggles, doubts, pains. Name a person of strong faith in the Bible – Abraham, David, Paul, even Jesus Himself – and they had to deal with difficult burdens. So yes, burdens are a reality in a world broken by sin. Even for Christians.

Second, we are reminded that God doesn't want His people to face burdens alone. "Bear one another's burdens." One of Satan's favorite tactics is to get us fighting alone. Look at David. David had been so faithful to God, from the shepherd fields to the throne of Israel. But one night Satan got him alone, away from his servants and his army, up on a rooftop, and tempted him, which led to David committing adultery with Bathsheba (2 Samuel 11:1-2). What about Peter? Peter had been so strong among the apostles, declaring to Jesus that "Even though all may fall away because of you, I will never fall away" (Matthew 26:33). But then Satan got him alone, away from Jesus and the apostles, where it wasn't popular to be a follower of Jesus, and he denied Jesus three times. Satan tried the same tactic on Jesus. When

Satan wanted to tempt Jesus most strongly, he got Him – guess where? – alone, away from the crowds in the wilderness (Matthew 4:1-11). Jesus didn't give in, but it's interesting that Satan thought his best chance to tempt Jesus was to get Jesus by Himself. That's what Satan wants to do: get us alone, get us fighting by ourselves. That's a battle Satan thinks he can win, and that's why we need fellow Christians to help us with our struggles.

One night my wife and I were watching one of those nature shows you see on TV from time to time. This one was in Africa, and the cameras were following some lions as they attempted to sneak up on a group of elephants. The narrator explained that even though elephants are much bigger than lions, the lions had a plan. The lions' goal was to create havoc among the elephants, to get them running, and then try to separate one single elephant from the group. The lions couldn't take on the entire group at once, but if they could get one elephant by himself, that's a battle they believed they could win. However, the elephants were pretty smart themselves, and when they realized that lions were threatening nearby, they formed a circle, with the smallest elephants in the center of the circle, and the larger elephants on the outside, facing outward to defend the group. The lions circled from a distance, looking for an opportunity, but eventually decided to leave. What a wonderful picture of what the church should be doing: circling up together against potential attacks, not giving Satan a chance to get anyone fighting by themselves. Bear one another's burdens.

Third, we are reminded that helping our fellow Christians through burdens is part of "fulfilling the law of Christ." We are supposed to have our own personal faith and closeness with God, but don't forget that part of following God also includes being there for our fellow Christians. You and I have a responsibility to each other as fellow believers.

So when Christians fall short of that responsibility – when we don't bear each other's burdens – what holds us back? I'm sure it's a combination of problems. First, in our self-centered culture, it's difficult for us to grasp the idea that we have responsibility for anyone else. So most people prefer to stand on their own, and they refuse to make time for any relationship that might slow them down on their path of pursuing personal life achievements. Second, sometimes we are "too busy" or too self-absorbed to even notice other people's burdens, or to even build relationships with fellow Christians at all. Third, many people become better at criticizing others for their burdens or competing pridefully with each other instead of building real relationships of mutual trust and support.

Perhaps you can name other problems that hold us back from fulfilling this part of our Christian responsibility. Whatever the problems, they are all rooted in sin, and so we must find ways to do better, to do what Christ wants us to do. Our faith isn't just about ourselves. Let's help bear each other's burdens, and thereby fulfill the law of Christ.

What We Must Do Better

So let's say that we commit ourselves to doing better. After all, this whole book has been about a commitment to being the church that God intended us to be. What must we do better to bear each other's burdens as fellow Christians?

First, we must commit ourselves to genuine Christian fellowship. How will we ever know about each other's burdens if we don't know each other well to begin with? The sad truth is that some Christians worship together for years without ever really knowing what's going on in each other's lives. That's not true of most churches I know, but it's more common than it should be.

This is where Christian fellowship – genuine fellowship and life-sharing – is so crucial for the church to become a real family. There is no replacement for time together. In Acts chapter 2, after 3000 people were baptized into Christ, notice their togetherness in Acts 2:42-47. Verse 44 says "And all those who had believed *were together* and had all things in common." Verse 46 says "*Day by day* continuing with one mind in the temple, and breaking bread *from house to house*, they were *taking their meals together* with gladness and sincerity of heart." The church at Jerusalem was together "day by day." They ate meals together. They worshiped together. They talked and shared with each other. There was genuine relationship between Christians, the type that can only come by spending time together.

When we have spent time together and built genuine relationships, then when something happens in my life, it's easier for me to share it with my fellow Christians. It's easier because they know my heart and my life, and I know theirs, so I can trust them to offer love and support as I work through difficult things. I know they will pray for me and encourage me. And who knows, since we are close, a fellow Christian might even notice something is wrong before I tell them. Sometimes sincerely asking if everything is OK, coming from someone who loves me, opens the door for the conversation we need to have. If we have true fellowship in the church, it becomes so much easier to talk to each other about our burdens. After all, when we have struggles, aren't we most likely to talk about them with the people we feel closest to?

That's why the church has so many events that point inwards, in order to build the sense of fellowship that produces genuine Christian life-sharing. Besides sharing things that are directly faith-related, such as Bible classes and worship services and service projects, you also find many activities that simply build closeness among Christians (just like that Jerusalem church in Acts 2:42-47). You will find potluck lunches after Sunday worship. You will find retreats and camps that include time to simply enjoy being together. You will find youth groups playing laser tag or going to the movies. You will find game nights and get-togethers in people's homes. What do these have to do with the church? They bring us into constant contact with other Christians, whose good examples help us desire to be stronger in faith ourselves. These fellowship activities also help build closeness among fellow believers, the type of closeness and love that produces a real support system for each other. That way, when burdens appear in the lives of Christians, their support system is ready to spring into action, and it's easier because genuine fellowship has already been built. Close Christian relationships make it so much easier to be a burden-bearing church family.

Second, we must commit ourselves to the effort it takes to help bear burdens. Relationships take time, and helping each other takes time also. Unfortunately, time is something that many people are not willing to sacrifice in our selfish, fast-paced culture. We must remember, this is part of the "law of Christ" (Gal. 6:2), so this is part of the church's responsibility. Notice some passages that talk about the time and effort required to bear each other's burdens:

- Romans 12:15 talks about the effort needed when Christians are in *times of difficulty or sadness*. It reads: "Rejoice with those who rejoice, and weep with those who weep." It doesn't just say "think about those who weep," it says to "weep with" them. We weep with fellow Christians by showing them we care. We get together with them to talk, to listen, to pray. We bring meals to help out and make sure they know we love them. We send cards of encouragement. We give hugs. We see what their needs are and try to help with them. We keep checking back. All these things take effort, but it's effort that is well worth it to help a fellow Christian hold up through difficult times.

- Matthew 18:15-17 talks about the effort needed when a fellow Christian is *struggling with sin*. When someone is getting tangled in sin, it is much easier to ignore the problem and avoid the difficult conversations, but that path leads toward allowing a soul to be lost (James 5:19-20). Sometimes it just takes a loving conversation with a godly friend to wake us up and get us back on the right path. In fact, that's exactly what happened to David, when his friend and fellow believer Nathan came to talk to him about his sin in 2 Samuel 12:1-13. Having conversations about the "real issues" is sometimes difficult, but it's well worth the effort to help a Christian get back on the path they know they need to be on.
- Romans 15:1-2 refers to the effort needed to *help Christians who are growing in their faith*. It says that "strong" Christians are supposed to help bear others' weaknesses of faith and knowledge. We are all sinful, and we are all growing (hopefully),

> so we must be patient with each other's growth process. Just as we know we should be patient with children who are growing physically and emotionally, we must also be patient with people are growing spiritually. I can say for myself, I'm so thankful for fellow Christians who overlooked my immaturity and encouraged me as I grew in faith. In fact, I'm thankful for the ones who are still overlooking my immaturities and encouraging me! None of us are finished products, and so we will always need the kindness and patience and love that are found in a church family.
>
> It takes effort to be patient with each other when we fail, or when we keep asking questions, or when we don't have our priorities right like we should. It takes effort to forgive each other (Eph. 4:32). It takes effort to seek those who have been drifting away from attending worship services. It takes effort to keep encouraging each other towards Christ. But all these things are efforts well spent to help a growing fellow Christian grow into a mature person of faith.

Bearing one another's burdens takes effort, but we must commit ourselves to whatever effort it requires to help each other get to heaven. Remember, just one soul is worth more than the whole world put together (Matthew 16:26) – any amount of effort is worth it!

The Church of Christ

God designed His church to live in relationship with each other. Our faith is not just about ourselves. God doesn't want us fighting sin or struggles on our own, and therefore we all need a family, a support system. And there is no greater support system than the family of God, working with God and with one another.

Don't you want to part of a church that really helps each other through life? A church that really encourages each other in faith? That's what God wants for us also. So how can we do better? Start with yourself: build relationships with fellow Christians. Be part of church fellowship activities and meet people you don't know well. Plan a church fellowship activity. Stay around after church services to talk and get to know people better. Show genuine love and interest to others. Reach out to those who are hurting. Pay attention to who hasn't been at services in awhile and let them know they are missed. Be an encourager.

If we want to be a church that pleases God, we need to put effort toward the "inward" operation of the church, encouraging each other in faith. Let's love God enough to be there for one another. "Bear one another's burdens, and thereby fulfill the law of Christ."

Discussion Questions

1) Do you think Christians have fewer burdens than non-Christians, or do you think they have more? Or is there no difference?
2) Name a person of strong faith in the Bible. Try to think of some burdens they had or struggles they faced.
3) How does Satan use our pride to get us fighting our spiritual battles alone?

4) What might keep Christians from bearing one another's burdens like we should? How could we do better?
5) What helps a church feel like a family? What holds a church back from feeling like a family?
6) How does it help our faith to have genuine friendships with other Christians?
7) What are some things Christians can do when fellow Christians are facing life difficulties?
8) Read John 13:34-35. From verse 35, name one way Jesus said people will know that the church is truly following Him. How does our love for each other help in Christian outreach to the world?
9) Read Philippians 2:1-4. How would these attitudes help Christians display unity and family? Read verses 5-11. How is Christ an example for how we should treat our fellow Christians?
10) Read Matthew 18:15-17. Why is it difficult to talk to others about sins that might be pulling them away from Christ? What attitudes must we have in those conversations? Read Galatians 6:1 for one example of the attitude God wants us to bring to conversations about sin and faith.
11) How must Christians show patience and forgiveness with each other? What happens if we don't?

Personal Reflection

1) Name some people in your church family who make you want to be a stronger Christian. What is it about them that encourages you? Can you do something similar to encourage someone else's faith?

2) Do you have a fellow Christian you can talk to openly and honestly about struggles and life difficulties? Don't let Satan use your pride to keep you fighting him by yourself!
3) Are you helping to build closeness in your church family? How? What more could you do personally to help your congregation be more of a family?

CHAPTER 10

God's Plan For Church Mission

"Go therefore and make disciples of all the nations, baptizing them in the name of the Father and the Son and the Holy Spirit, teaching them to observe all that I commanded you; and lo, I am with you always, even to the end of the age."
-Jesus to the apostles, in Matthew 28:19-20

Starters

- Do you remember the three directions God wants His church to act? What are they?
- Do you agree or disagree: The church has the world's most important mission. Why or why not?
- What was the mission of Jesus in coming to earth? (Read Luke 19:10 for a good "mission statement" from Jesus.) What are some ways that Jesus reached out to the world?
- If you were not a Christian, what might lead you to become a Christian? Imagine how that process might

happen: would you need to hear something? Meet someone? What might get you interested in Christianity?

A Life-Mission Worth Pursuing

People often search for a "life-mission" worth pursuing. They feel like there should be something deeper and more meaningful in life, and so they try all sorts of things in search of their "purpose." They try changing jobs. They try traveling the world. They try gaining more attention or chasing bigger worldly achievements. They seek a cause they can support or be passionate about. I suppose those are all interesting pursuits, but as life-missions, they still come up feeling somewhat empty.

You have probably spent time reflecting on what your purpose in life should be, trying to decide what is really worth your best focus and effort. From a biblical perspective, that desire for meaning and purpose is rooted in the fact that we are created for something bigger than this temporary world. As Ecclesiastes 3:11 puts it, God has "set eternity in our hearts," so that we have an inner desire for something bigger than this world can offer. Earthly activities may give short, temporary feelings of accomplishment, but the only things that can truly fulfill our inner desire for mission and purpose are spiritual things, eternal things.

Christians, of all people, should have the clearest understanding of eternal things, and therefore the clearest sense of life's most important mission. We of all people should understand that sin is the world's biggest problem, the problem that has ruined everything. We of all people should understand that life is temporary, and that we are all making decisions that will affect our eternity beyond this world.

And we of all people should realize that the only answers to those issues of sin and eternity – life's deepest issues and biggest concerns, whether the world realizes it or not – are found in Jesus Christ. So if spiritual and eternal things are the most important ones to pursue, we find life's most important purpose in the eternal, spiritual mission of Christ and His church.

The one true God is a God of mission, and He built His church with certain goals in mind. As we described it in the last chapter, God wants His church to operate upwards, inwards, and outwards. It takes energy and effort – and God's help – for the church to do all three, but all three are essential if the church is to be what God intended it to be. We operate upwards in worshiping God, loving God, and living in ways that honor God. We operate inwards by encouraging each other in faith and bearing one another's life burdens. In this chapter, we will think about how the church should operate *outwards*: the church should be reaching out to the world with the mission of Jesus. So what is the mission of Jesus, and how should we be pursuing it as a church?

The Mission of Jesus

Like everything else in the church, our mission begins with Jesus. Jesus is God from all eternity, but He was willing to leave the glory of heaven to be born as a man and live on earth (Phil. 2:5-11). Why? Jesus summarized His mission in a conversation with Zaccheus in Luke 19:10: "For the Son of Man has come to seek and to save that which was lost." Because of sin, we are a world full of souls who have "lost" our direction and relationship with God, and God loved us enough for Jesus to come "seek" and "save" us. It was a mission focused outward, on a world that needed to see the love and salvation of God.

So how did Jesus carry out His mission of seeking and saving the lost? Since Jesus is our example for living (1 John 2:6), let's start by seeing what He did to reach out and change lives.

- ***Jesus taught people God's word and how to live for Him.*** Matthew 4:23 describes this part of Jesus' ministry: "Jesus was going throughout all Galilee, *teaching* in their synagogues and *proclaiming the gospel* of the kingdom, ..." Jesus taught how we must live to be pleasing to God. He taught about God's kingdom, as both the church on earth and the eternal home with God. He taught about sin and hell and judgment. He taught about money and humility and sexual morality. He taught about repentance and baptism and evangelism. The list goes on. Teaching and preaching God's word was a centerpiece of Jesus' outreach-focused mission.
- ***Jesus showed people the love of God by helping them and doing good.*** Notice how Matthew 4:23 continues, still describing Jesus' ministry: "Jesus was going throughout all Galilee, teaching in their synagogues and proclaiming the gospel of the kingdom, and *healing every kind of disease and every kind of sickness among the people.*" Another common theme of Jesus' ministry was compassion for people and helping people. He healed lepers and blind men and paralytics. Even beyond His powers to heal, Jesus' ability to show a genuine love for people seems to be one reason that even sinners wanted to be around Him and wanted to listen to Him! (See Luke 15:1-2.)

- ***Jesus showed people a life example of what it means to truly live for God***. Jesus shows the world the goodness and character of God (John 1:18), and so we see in Him what a true godly life looks like. He didn't just tell people how to live right, He showed them. Jesus' genuine godly life is another reason people were drawn to Him, and why His words "Follow Me" were so compelling and life-transforming (Matthew 4:19, 9:9).
- ***Jesus helped others carry on His mission***. Jesus spent special time with the twelve men known as the apostles, allowing them to absorb His message and mission in a special way. He would send them out on smaller missions of teaching and healing (in Matthew chapter 10, for example), preparing them for the time after Jesus' return to heaven, when they would be ready take His mission to the world.
- ***Jesus went to the cross as a sacrifice for our sins***. In the ultimate act of sacrifice, Jesus went through the painful death on the cross, paying the price for our salvation that we could not pay ourselves. As 2 Corinthians 5:21 says it, "He made Him who knew no sin to be sin on our behalf, so that we might become the righteousness of God in Him."

Jesus' coming to earth was missional, an outreach from God to bring lost souls back to Him. Everything He did had that goal in mind. Jesus could have done lots of things with His life – become wealthy, traveled the world – but His life shows us that He believed the most important mission was eternal and spiritual: helping souls come back to God so they could be saved.

Jesus' Mission is His Church's Mission

Jesus taught that His followers were to join in His mission of reaching out to the world. In the Sermon on the Mount, for example, Jesus taught that His disciples were not to hide away from the world, but instead they were to impact the world with the salt and light of the gospel of God:

"You are the salt of the earth; but if the salt has become tasteless, how can it be made salty again? It is no longer good for anything, except to be thrown out and trampled under foot by men. You are the light of the world. A city set on a hill cannot be hidden; nor does anyone light a lamp and put it under a basket, but on the lampstand, and it gives light to all who are in the house. Let your light shine before men in such a way that they may see your good works, and glorify your Father who is in heaven."
-Jesus, in Matthew 5:14-16

And after Jesus was raised from the dead, He gave the apostles what is often called "The Great Commission," meaning their great "assignment" going forward as followers of Jesus:

And Jesus came up and spoke to them, saying, "All authority has been given to Me in heaven and on earth. Go therefore and make disciples of all the nations, baptizing them in the name of the Father and the Son and the Holy Spirit, teaching them to observe all that I commanded you; and lo, I am with you always, even to the end of the age."
-Jesus, in Matthew 28:18-20

You can never accuse Jesus of not having enough vision! That's about as big a vision as possible – "make disciples of *all the nations*" – and I wouldn't be surprised if the apostles wondered if it was even possible. But don't miss the end of that passage: they wouldn't be alone, they would have the help and strength of Jesus with them in their mission. Jesus gave the apostles the same global vision of outreach in Acts 1:8, telling them, "you shall be My witnesses both in Jerusalem, and in all Judea and Samaria, and even to the remotest part of the earth." Jesus had brought salvation to the world, and now He was handing His apostles the mission of sharing it with others.

That mission, of course, wouldn't stop with the apostles. As you read through the Book of Acts, you see all Christians taking part in Christian outreach. The church in Jerusalem quickly grew to over 5000 (Acts 4:4). And when persecution scattered Christians out of Jerusalem, did they run and hide? Of course not. "Those who were scattered went about preaching the word" (Acts 8:4). Outreach is part of the Christian DNA (remember, it began with Jesus Himself), and even persecution couldn't stop them from continuing the all-important mission of Jesus. Christianity would spread all over the Roman empire, and it wasn't long until people were referring to Christians as the ones "who have turned the world upside down" (Acts 17:6, ESV). The mission of Jesus had truly become the mission of His church, just as God planned.

How Does the Church Continue the Outreach Mission of Jesus Today?

So the church's "outwards" role is to continue the global vision and outreach-mission of Jesus. God's love led to Jesus' mission of seeking and saving the lost. Our love for God and for others leads us to share God's mission of reaching out to the world. So how does God want His church to be reaching out? Well, as followers of Jesus, we reach out in the same ways Jesus did:

- **Just like Jesus, the church should try to teach and share God's word.** The church shares the message of the gospel with the world: that sinners like us can receive salvation and new life through obeying Jesus Christ. But people can't receive salvation if they don't hear about it! As Romans 10:17 says, "So faith comes from hearing, and hearing by the word of Christ." Like Jesus, the church must give opportunities for people to hear God's word, praying that they will respond in obedient faith. And so the church teaches the Bible regularly and invites the world to come study along with us. The church also searches for ways to get God's word out into the world, through websites and television programs and books and magazines and tracts, giving people a chance to see God's word for themselves.

  And just like in the Bible, individual Christians also try to encourage others to think about their faith and their soul. In Acts 8:4, many Christians were "preaching the word" by talking about it to others when they had the opportunity. One great example is in Acts 8:26-38, where Philip has a faith conversation with an Ethiopian nobleman, which leads to the nobleman being baptized into Christ. Like those Christians in the Bible, we seek to discuss faith and encourage people to follow Jesus. 1 Peter 3:15 says Christians should have those conversations in a spirit of "gentleness and reverence" (not a spirit of anger or arrogance). Christians know we have the most important message in the world, and so the church's outreach includes teaching, just like Jesus.

- **Just like Jesus, the church should try to help others and do good out of genuine love**. Jesus said that the second-greatest command is to love our neighbor as ourselves (Matthew 22:36-40). So following the example of Jesus, the church reaches out by showing kindness and love to all people, including the poor and the hurting. Churches have food pantries and clothes closets and service projects, and Christians constantly look for ways to help others. Like Jesus, sometimes our service leads to opportunities for teaching the gospel, and sometimes it is simply an opportunity to show the goodness and love of God in action. Galatians 6:10 says "So then, while we have opportunity, *let us do good to all people*, and especially to those who are of the household of faith." Christian outreach includes showing God's love to the world through service and helping those who are hurting, just like Jesus did.
- **Just like Jesus, the church should try to show the world a genuine example of what it means to live for God**. Though we will never fully get there, Christians try to live like Jesus (1 John 2:6, 1 Corinthians 11:1). By living in a way that genuinely tries to follow God, we are showing the world the goodness of the Christian life, and we provide a living sermon of how God can transform sinners into people of sincere faith (not perfect faith, but sincere faith). Christians should talk differently from the world. They should treat people differently. They should respond to problems and their own failures differently. In all these ways and many others, Christian examples shine the light of Christ. As Paul told Timothy in 1 Timothy 4:12, "in speech, conduct, love, faith, and purity, show yourself *an example* of those who believe." There is plenty of religious hypocrisy in the world, and some-

times people simply need to see a "real" Christian to seriously consider following Jesus themselves. Christian outreach includes showing the world what it means to truly live for God, just like Jesus did.

- **Just like Jesus, the church should try to help others effectively carry the mission of Jesus forward**. Jesus trained the apostles to take the gospel to the world, and so the church continues to train and prepare each other to better reach out. In 2 Timothy 2:2, Paul wrote, "The things which you have heard from me in the presence of many witnesses, entrust these to faithful men who will be able to teach others also." The church teaches one another, and encourages one another to share the gospel with the world. So the church has evangelism classes and youth-training programs and encourages Christians to use their talents to impact the world for Christ. Also, the church helps financially support those who want to devote their life to sharing the gospel: the church supports preachers and ministers and missionaries and other good outreach efforts all over the world. As 3 John 8 says, when the church supports those who devote their lives to sharing the gospel, they are "fellow workers with the truth."

The Church of Christ

Sometimes churches never build a true outreach perspective. Maybe they think they are too insignificant and don't think their outreach will make a difference. Maybe they are struggling with internal problems, keeping them from having the energy to reach out until they can find better inner stability. Maybe they just don't know what to do. But if we are going to truly be the church of Christ we see in the Bible, we must find ways to do what Christ wanted us to do, and that includes reaching out to our world – starting with our own communities – with the light and love of God.

Jesus' life was a life of mission, and Jesus wanted His church to continue the mission He began, seeking and saving the lost. Jesus paid the price for sin on the cross, and church shares that messages by continuing the ways Jesus reached out to the world: teaching God's word, showing God's love, living godly lives, and helping support one another in outreach. The church in the New Testament did those things, and with the help of God, the Roman empire soon felt like the world had been turned upside down. The gospel of Christ has continued to change lives around the world ever since, and today the church must prayerfully continue that outreach-perspective. Jesus brought the greatest message and mission the world has ever known. With the help of God, let's show our world the wonderful gift offered in Christ, a message that "holds promise for the present life and also for the life to come" (1 Timothy 4:8).

What's Next...

In these last three chapters, we have seen God's desire for the church to live out His plan in three different directions. The church is supposed to operate *upwards* in worship and transformed living, *inwards* in faith encouragement, and *outwards* in missional outreach. We must never forget the big picture of what God wanted His church to do! Let's make sure we're pursuing all three as best we can.

The next section is entitled "Keeping Perspective in a Divided Religious World." We have talked a lot in this book about trying to simply be Christians, as the one church of Christ that God established in Scripture, doing things God's way. I believe those are the right goals, the ones we find in the Bible. However, not everyone in our religious world shares those goals, and many haven't even heard about them yet. The result? Trying to do things God's way can cause unintended friction with those who don't agree or don't want to change from "the way we already do things." I suppose trying to do things God's way has always caused friction, but it's still not easy whenever we see disagreement in those around us. It can be difficult to maintain a Christ-centered, Scripture-centered perspective amidst a complex and divided religious world. How can we keep the right perspective? That will be our study in the next two chapters...

Discussion Questions

1) What are some of the themes Jesus preached on? Did He only preach on "happy topics?" Did He only preach on "unhappy topics?" How should Jesus' example affect how we preach today?
2) Why do you think the apostles were willing to leave their jobs and follow Jesus when He asked them? (Matthew 4:19, 9:9)
3) How do you think the apostles felt when Jesus gave them the task of taking the gospel to the entire world in Matthew 28:18-20? How would you have felt? That makes Jesus' promise in verse 20, "I am with you always," even more special and needed, doesn't it?
4) Of the different forms of church outreach mentioned in this chapter, which do you think is the most difficult? Which is easiest? Will the answers be different

for different people? We will all have different roles, but we all try to reach out together as a church!

5) What are some ways the church can share the teachings of the Bible with their community?
6) What does 1 Peter 3:15 say about the attitudes we should have in talking to others about faith? What about 2 Timothy 2:24-26? How would these attitudes change the tone of our religious conversations? Do you think they would cause people to be more open to talking and listening?
7) Looking around your community, what open doors might there be for showing the love of God by helping others? How could the church act on those open doors?
8) Will everyone helped by Christians become a Christian or even have interest? Will they all be thankful? Should we show them God's kindness anyway? (See Luke 17:11-19 for an example from the life of Jesus.)
9) In what situations might Christians struggle to be a good example for Christ?
10) Christian examples will never be perfect. So how can Christians respond to their failures in ways that still show a genuine faith and desire to follow God?
11) Sometimes churches get so excited about outreach that they are willing to change or ignore God's teachings to be more accepted and try to increase their numbers. Did Jesus want His followers to change God's word in order to please culture or people? Did the apostles or the church in the Bible think we should change God's word to be more popular?

12) Does your church support any preachers or missionaries outside of your congregation? Who and where? How did that partnership begin?
13) How can the church better train and encourage each other in our outreach?
14) What keeps churches from having the outreach perspective God wants them to have? How can churches do better?

Personal Reflection

1) Do you agree that the mission of Christ is the most important mission we can put our time into? There are certainly other things in life that require your time, but how can you make sure you put plenty of time and effort into that most important mission?
2) What areas of church outreach can you help with? Pray about it and get involved in God's outreach mission!
3) How comfortable am I in talking with people about religion and faith? How can I grow in this area? How can I do it in a way that lets others know I truly care about them as individuals?
4) Are there certain places in your life where you struggle to be the Christian example you should be? What causes the struggle? How can you do better? Pray about it, and let your light shine for Christ!

Section 4:
Keeping Perspective in a Divided Religious World

CHAPTER 11

The Church In A Divided Religious World: Keeping Perspective On Our Goals

"but so that the world may know that I love the Father,
I do exactly as the Father commanded Me."
-Jesus, in John 14:31

Starters

- What are some of the challenges of teaching undenominational Christianity in our divided religious world?
- Do people sometimes misunderstand the undenominational goals of the churches of Christ? What do you think they misunderstand? How could we make our goals more clear?
- Some people criticize the idea of trying to get everything right in the church's teaching and practice. Any

guesses why someone might criticize that? What would you say in response?

Keeping Perspective in a Divided Religious World

It's been a consistent theme in this book, and it's true: we live in a divided and complex religious world. There are so many different beliefs and ideas – even among people who are professing to follow Jesus – that it can be difficult to get a handle on what God really wants from His people. That doesn't mean we stop trying to find God's way; in fact, it means we must strive even more diligently to seek, find, and obey God's plan.

The good news about finding ourselves in a divided religious world: God's plan has been in divided religious worlds before and done just fine. In fact, the Roman world of New Testament times was extremely complex and divided, with innumerable idols and "gods" along with a wide range of philosophies and religious practices. God's plan prospered anyway, with the gospel spreading all over the world. So the good news is that God's plan has a history of rising to the top in spite of the many competing religious options. All it takes is people who are willing to trust God and obey His plan.

The bad news? Divided religious worlds produce friction and disagreement, even for those who are trying to do the right thing. As the apostles went out sharing God's plan in the Book of Acts, they faced a lot of opposition. Some people got upset because they expected to lose money if God's plan kept spreading (Acts 19:23-27). Some people were simply upset that God's plan was different from the beliefs they had long held, and they didn't want to change (Acts 19:23-27 again). Some people reacted against God's plan because they were jealous of the attention it was getting (Acts 17:5). Some people had heard incorrectly what the apostles were doing, and so they reacted angrily without really understanding their message (Acts 21:27-30). Were the apostles teaching anything wrong? Of course not – the problem wasn't the message. The problem is that all of us get ingrained in our religious beliefs, and if we're not careful, we naturally push back against anything that's different, even if it's right.

So let's say that you and I decide we will really try to follow God's plan for His church. We avoid denominational names, taking only the name of Christ. We start teaching and practicing God's word only, refusing to let man-made traditions hold us back. We strive for the church to operate God's way in all three directions God wants: upward, inward, and outward. I believe we would be doing the right thing and following God's plan for His church. But guess what? We would still find ourselves in the middle of a complex religious world, surrounded by a lot of other people who aren't pursuing those goals of undenominational Christianity. And that's going to produce friction, even if the message is the right one. Can we handle that friction in the Christ-like way God desires?

That's the question of this chapter and the next chapter, which are both about keeping perspective in a divided religious world. That can be difficult, for at least two reasons. First, when people are moving in such different directions, it's easy to get bumped around in the crowd and lose track of where we are trying to go. We must regularly look up to make sure we haven't gotten distracted by what everyone else is saying and doing, and check to see that we are still going in the right direction spiritually. Second, it's difficult to keep perspective in a divided religious world because of that friction we have mentioned – people often pushback against anything that is different from what they've always been taught. That pushback can result in argumentative and competitive relationships if we are not careful. So making sure we keep the right perspective on our goals is important, and so is keeping the right perspective on the message we want to share with our religious neighbors. Let's consider those ideas, in the rest of this chapter and the next one.

Why Are You So Concerned With Getting Everything Right?

Two young ladies, close friends, have been discussing faith and church. Samantha grew up worshiping with the East Street Church of Christ, while Lisa grew up attending a denominational congregation a few streets over. They have been friends since middle school, and every now and then – in between homework, trips to the mall, and laughing at videos on their phones – Samantha and Lisa have discussed their different religious backgrounds. They grew up going to church with their families, but now that they are in college, they have begun asking their own questions, trying to decide what is right, knowing that they are getting a little older and need to take more responsibility for their own faith decisions. Faith and church have always been part of their families and their lives, so it has never been an awkward conversation topic for them; their friendship has made it easy to discuss, despite the differences in their church upbringings. Their last conversation about growing up and making their own faith decisions turned into a deeper discussion about the goals of the churches of Christ: trying to simply be the church Christ established, and following the

Bible as closely as possible in making the church the way God wanted it.

Lisa had always gone to a different church, but she couldn't stop thinking about what she heard from Samantha in that last conversation. It made so much sense to her to go back to the New Testament, and to get rid of all the things men had added through the years: the denominational names and denominational handbooks and people-centered worship practices. To simply be Christians without the historical baggage seemed like the obvious right thing to do. She began to wonder: why doesn't everyone think that way? Finally, Lisa went to talk to the preacher at the denominational church she had grown up in. As Lisa began to share some of her thoughts, her preacher interrupted and responded in a way that took Lisa by surprise. He said that God wants the church to focus on Jesus, and not spend time on smaller matters of trying to get everything right. He said it sounded to him like the churches of Christ were being legalistic, meaning they were trying to earn their salvation by trying to do everything right. He said trying to get everything right was too much like the Pharisees, criticizing everyone else and being proud of their own rule-following. These were all new thoughts to Lisa – she had never gotten that impression from Samantha or her family – so after thanking the preacher for his time and thoughts, her mind began spinning as she drove home.

The conversation with her preacher was now the one running through Lisa's head, and she decided she had to discuss it with Samantha. The goals of churches of Christ had sounded so good to her, but now she began to wonder: is it wrong for churches of Christ to be concerned with trying to get everything right? Are they just trying to make themselves out to be better than everyone else? Lisa really liked the idea of just being a Christian, the way they were in the Bible, but she didn't want to become part of something that was more focused on rules than on Jesus. She parked her car at Samantha's place, and couldn't wait to ask her: why are churches of Christ so concerned with getting everything right?

If you were Samantha, what would you say to that question? Sometimes our religious neighbors misunderstand what we're trying to do in pursuing undenominational Christianity. I'm sure part of that is our fault for not sharing our goals in the right way. They hear what I believe is the right message, but they sometimes hear it as too critical or too arrogant or too legalistic. I believe that trying to get everything right for God is the right goal, but let's make sure we understand why we pursue it – and why we don't...

What We Are NOT Doing

Perhaps it would help to start by making clear what we are *not* doing when we decide to try to make the church everything God wants it to be:

First, we are not being legalistic, trying to save ourselves by "getting everything right." Ephesians 2:9 is one place where the Bible clearly states our salvation is "not as a result of works, so that no one may boast." Salvation is given to us only by the grace of God through Jesus Christ, so whatever our motives are (which we will see in just a second), they are not some attempt to save ourselves by our own perfection. All men are sinners before God (Romans 3:23), and therefore we all depend on Christ's blood for salvation. Does God want us to obey Him and try to do things

His way? Yes He does, but not with the motive of saving ourselves by our own goodness or faultlessness.

Second, in trying to make the church everything God wants it to be, we are not trying to lift ourselves up as somehow "better" than anyone else. This was indeed one of the mistakes the Pharisees made during Jesus' life. The Pharisees spent a lot of time trying to glorify themselves, wanting people to think of them as much holier and more knowledgeable than everyone else. As a result, the Pharisees became faultfinders, relishing opportunities to point out where others fell short. Whether it was following Jesus into a grain field to accuse Him (Matthew 12:1-2), or dragging a woman before a crowd to publicly debate her sinfulness (John 8:1-11), or throwing a man out of the synagogue for daring to tell them that they might be wrong about Jesus (John 9:30-34), the Pharisees had developed a sad habit of criticizing everyone else's faith. Does God want us to talk with each other and show each other where we might be sinning or missing His will? Yes He does, and we probably need to have those conversations more than we do, but not with an attitude of trying to make ourselves better than everyone else.

So if those are *not* the reasons we try to get everything right in the church, why *do* we try to get everything right in the church?

Keeping Our Motives Right

Why are we concerned with trying to get everything right in the church, from teachings on the Bible and salvation to teachings on leadership and worship, and beyond? If our motives are where they should be, it all begins with a genuine love for God. We see God's love toward us through Jesus

Christ, and we respond in love toward the God who made us and wants to save us. And as we read the teachings of Jesus, we notice some things that He says naturally flow from loving God:

"but so that the world may know that I love the Father, I do ***exactly*** *as the Father commanded Me."*
-Jesus, in John 14:31

Jesus' love for the Father produced the goal of doing exactly – notice that word – as the Father commanded. Jesus didn't want to do "sort of" what the Father commanded, or "most of" what the Father commanded. He wanted to do "exactly" what the Father commanded. Was Jesus being legalistic or trying to be better than everyone else? Of course not. It came from where He said it came from: showing the world how much He loved the Father.

A few verses before, in John 14:23-24, Jesus said that our love for God will be shown in the same way, in how much we obey His word:

"If anyone loves Me, he will keep My word; and My Father will love him, and We will come to him and make Our abode with him. He who does not love Me does not keep My words; and the word which you hear is not Mine, but the Father's who sent Me."
-Jesus, in John 14:23-24

Jesus says there is a direct correlation between how much we love God and how much we obey His words. That makes sense, because if I see anything in God's word – whether I think it is a big matter or a small matter – and I decide I'd rather do things my way instead of God's, I have a heart problem. Why else would I see God's plan and still decide on a different path? My heart is choosing sin and self over God. But if I love God, I will desire to please Him in all things, so when I see His word on any matter – big or small – I do my best to obey it and do it His way. So when we try to be a church that follows God's plan in all things, we should be doing it out of a genuine love for God, which produces obedience to all of His words.

Look also at how Jesus described becoming a disciple in Matthew 28:19-20:

> *"Go therefore and make disciples of all the nations, baptizing them in the name of the Father and the Son and the Holy Spirit, teaching them to observe all that I commanded you; and lo, I am with you always, even to the end of the age."*
> *-Jesus, in Matthew 28:19-20*

Jesus mentioned two steps here in "making disciples." First He mentions baptism, which we studied back in chapter six. But notice the second step: teaching those who are baptized to observe "all" that I commanded you. Followers of Jesus don't settle for doing "some" or "most" of what Jesus commanded, they try to observe "all" that He commanded. Was Jesus telling His disciples to be legalistic or to act like they were better than everyone else? Of course not. Trying to do everything right for God has much better motives than that: following the example and teachings of Jesus, we do it out of a genuine love for God and a genuine desire to follow Christ in all that He commanded.

Keeping Our Emphasis Right

Sometimes our religious neighbors ask a similar question about trying to get everything right, but with a different twist: Doesn't God want us to just focus on the major things in Scripture and not worry about the smaller things? They may point to a passage like Matthew 23:23, where Jesus had some strong words for the Pharisees:

> *"Woe to you, scribes and Pharisees, hypocrites! For you tithe mint and dill and cummin, and have neglected the weightier provisions of the law: justice and mercy and faithfulness; but these are the things you should have done without neglecting the others."*
> *-Jesus, in Matthew 23:23*

Under the Old Testament Law of Moses, the Israelites were supposed to tithe, meaning give ten percent of their wealth to God's work. And the Pharisees were being so meticulous about tithing that they were even tithing their household spices! Jesus is upset at them for putting effort into doing something small like tithing spices, while missing some bigger matters like justice and mercy and faithfulness.

That's a great passage, and it does teach us at least two things. First, it does teach that some things are more important than others. Jesus says there are some "weightier matters" in God's law, things that need to be emphasized and encouraged more than other things. That's true in the Christian faith, isn't it? Paul would later say that Jesus' death for our sins, burial, and resurrection are "of first importance" in the teachings of Christianity (1 Corinthians 15:1-4). We also see the idea that some things are more important than others in Matthew 22:36-40, when they asked Jesus which was the greatest commandment. Jesus didn't say "there is no commandment greater than another." Instead, He answered that loving God with our whole lives is the first commandment, and the second commandment is to love your neighbor as yourself. So yes, it's true, some things are more important than others in the Bible, and we must keep the emphasis where God wants it. We must emphasize the death and resurrection of Jesus. We must emphasize loving God and loving our neighbor. We must keep first things first.

But don't miss the second thing that Jesus teaches us in Matthew 23:23. After criticizing the Pharisees for getting small things right while getting big things wrong, Jesus says, "these are the things you should have done without neglecting the others." The problem was *not* that the Pharisees were obeying small things like tithing their spices. Jesus doesn't criticize them for trying to obey God in the small things. The problem was that they were focusing on the little things while missing the big things – and Jesus says they should have been doing *both*! That tells us that even though some things should be emphasized more than others in God's law, *every* word and command of God is still important.

We see that same principle in Matthew 22:36-40. After Jesus gave the first and second commands of loving God and loving our neighbor, notice what He then said in verse 40: "On these two commandments depend the whole Law and the Prophets." Jesus wanted His followers to get first things first, but He knew that getting the first two commandments right would then naturally produce a life that would obey all the rest of God's law too. Some commands are of first importance, but all of God's commands are important.

The Bible never teaches that God wants us only to focus on the big things, and that the smaller things in God's plan are just optional extras. Yes, there are some things that should be emphasized in the Christian faith. But followers of Jesus, out of a love for God, should seek to know and obey God's will in every matter, big and small. How should we worship? Whether you think that's a big matter or a small matter, a person of faith will seek God's answer and follow it. How should we organize leadership of God's church? Whether you think that's a big matter or a small matter, a person of faith will seek God's answer and follow it. And whenever we see God's word on something and we just decide not to follow it, even if we think it's a "smaller issue," we have a heart problem, because we are choosing our way over God's. In trying to follow all of God's plan for the church, we're trying to honor all of God's teachings. Some things should indeed be emphasized more than others. But big, small, and everywhere in between, God wants us to follow His word.

The Church of Christ

Our divided religious world can sometimes make it difficult to keep perspective on what we're trying to be. We need to make sure we understand our goals clearly, so that we can explain them clearly when we get the opportunities. In trying to follow all of God's plan for His church, we are not trying to save ourselves by our own works, and we are not trying to portray ourselves as better than anyone else. We try to pursue undenominational Christianity out of deeper and better motives: out of a true love for God and true desire to be a follower of Jesus. We honor God whenever we try to get everything right for Him, not just the big things and certainly not just the small things. Let's keep first things first, but let's continue to seek and follow God's will in all our teachings and practices.

Years ago, I sat in a Wednesday night Bible class of about 75 college students. I don't remember how it started, but the teacher began sharing with us how he came to be serving as a minister in the churches of Christ. He had grown up in a denominational church, and he met some people who worshiped at a local church of Christ. After hearing about some of their teachings on things like baptism and worship and being undenominational, he said that he "set out to prove the church of Christ wrong." He studied and read for himself. He looked at all sides of the issues. By the end of his long personal study, he had entirely switched course. He was baptized into Christ, and committed himself to practicing Christianity the way it was taught and practiced in the New Testament. Now he was serving as a minister in the church, helping college age students pursue those same goals. But I loved how he described that process, looking back at it. He said: "I set out to prove the church of Christ wrong, and instead, I proved God right." In other words, he didn't "prove the church of Christ right." In reality, this wasn't (and must never be) a competition between the church of Christ and any other religious group. The goal was to find God's will and to follow it.

Our divided religious world tempts people to think in a competitive way, but just trying to 'be right' or 'be better' than someone else are not the goals of God's people, and so they must never be our goals. We are simply trying to seek God's will and follow it. Big, small, and in between. We would love for everyone else to do the same. Not to prove one group right and another group wrong, but for all of us together to prove God right. Let's give God everything He wants in His church, not only doing the right things, but doing them for the right reasons as well.

What's Next...

In this chapter, we've tried to study the proper perspective on our goals. In the next chapter, we will continue to reflect on our place in a divided religious world, by studying a proper perspective on our religious neighbors. As we've said, we are surrounded by people who think and practice differently than we do. How should we treat our religious neighbors, including the many who haven't yet seen the goodness of simply being undenominational Christians? How did the early Christians treat their religious neighbors in the New Testament? Can we learn something from them? It can be difficult to engage a divided religious world in the right way. I pray our study in the next chapter will be helpful.

Discussion Questions

1) Is it possible for Christians to be more focused on rules than on Jesus? If so, how can we make sure it's never about rules more than Jesus?
2) Does getting everything right in our church's teaching and practice save us? If not, what saves us?
3) If getting everything right doesn't save us, are there still certain things God has told us to do to receive salvation through Christ?
4) If getting everything right doesn't save us, should we still try to get everything right? Why or why not? Did Jesus try to get everything right for God? (Look back at John 14:31.)
5) What were some mistakes the Pharisees made in their attempts to follow God? Can Christians sometimes make the same mistakes today?
6) What are the right motives for trying to get everything right in following God's plan for His church?

7) Do you think any church will ever be perfect? In chapter 3, we talked about the difference between (a) an imperfect church that is striving to follow God's plan to the best of its ability and (b) an imperfect church that has no real desire to change where it is different from God's plan. Do you agree that there's a difference between those two?

8) Are there some teachings that need to be emphasized more than others in Christianity? What passages of Scripture talk about "first" teachings?

9) If some teachings are more important than others, does that mean we should not care whether we get the "lesser" teachings right? What passages encourage trying to obey in all things? What was Jesus' attitude about obedience in big and small matters?

10) Does our divided religious world tempt us to make religious beliefs a competition? How can we help conversations with our religious neighbors be less competitive and more about seeking the truth?

Personal Reflection

1) Read Jesus' parable about the Pharisee and the tax collector in Luke 18:9-14. How can I make sure my religious attitude never becomes like the Pharisee's?

2) Doing the right things for the right reasons can sometimes be difficult. Is there a time I have done the right thing, but for the wrong reason? How can I purify my motives to do it for the right reason next time? Read 1 Samuel 16:7 for a reminder about how important it is to purify our motives and hearts.

3) In John 14:23-24, Jesus says that our love for God will produce obedience. What are some ways I can deepen my love for God? In what ways do I need to give greater obedience to God?

CHAPTER 12

The Church In A Divided Religious World: Keeping Perspective On Our Religious Neighbors

"Now while Paul was waiting for them at Athens, his spirit was being provoked within him as he was observing the city full of idols. So he was reasoning in the synagogue with the Jews and the God-fearing Gentiles, and in the market place every day with those who happened to be present."
-Acts 17:16-17

Starters

- Do you think Christians should be trying to encourage our religious neighbors to follow Christ? How can we do that? What are some things that make it difficult?

- Have you ever seen a religious conversation turn into an argument? Why did that happen? What could have been done better to avoid an argument?
- Our culture tells us that everyone is okay no matter what they believe. Does the Bible support that idea?
- How would you describe the way Christians interacted with their religious neighbors in the Book of Acts? Did they hide what they believed? Did they say that everyone was okay no matter what they believed?

How to Approach a Divided Religious World?

In the last chapter, we saw that our divided religious world can sometimes muddy the waters, making it difficult to keep perspective on who God wants His people to be. But even after we firmly establish our goals of simply being Christians and following God's plan, trying to do the right things for the right reasons, some challenges still remain. One of the biggest challenges of a divided religious world is our relationship to those who have different religious practices. Some questions we ask: What is our message to those who seem sincere in their faith and seem like "good people," but don't follow Jesus? What is our relationship with those who consider themselves Christians, yet do things so differently from the Bible's teachings? Are people who have different religious practices our enemies? Our allies? Should we be sharing God's plan for the church with them? Should we just say that everyone's okay and ignore our differences? The questions can leave us dizzy, wondering where to start.

Well, we have some great starting points in our New Testament, because as the last chapter reminded us, Christians in the first century had to engage a very divided religious world also. The first-century Roman world had a wide variety of philosophies, religions, idols, and religious practices. Perhaps the early Christians asked the same questions we are asking about how to share Christ's message among so many people who believed differently. We see in their example that Christianity has faced the challenge of bringing the message of Jesus to a complex religious world before, and has done very well. How did they do it? In this chapter, we will look around the New Testament to see how God's church interacted with people who were at different places in their religious faith. I hope it will help us clarify in our minds how we should view and interact with our religious neighbors today.

Things to Remember First

Let's start by mentioning a few commitments we must be sure to keep in our minds, commitments that will affect our relationship with our religious neighbors:

First, we must make sure we are applying God's words to ourselves. Before we start thinking about sharing God's plan with others, they must first see that we are sincere enough to apply it to ourselves. Remember what Jesus said in Matthew 7:3-5:

> *"Why do you look at the speck that is in your brother's eye, but do not notice the log that is in your own eye? Or how can you say to your brother, 'Let me take the speck out of your eye,' and behold, the log is in your own eye? You hypocrite, first take the log out of your own eye, and then you will see clearly to take the speck out of your brother's eye."*

Jesus is condemning those who want to tell everyone else what they're doing wrong without genuinely trying to live for God themselves. Jesus calls those people the same thing we call them today: hypocrites (verse 5). But notice exactly what Jesus is saying in verse 5: He does *not* say that we should stop trying to help others get the speck out of their eye, He just says that we *first* need to get the log out of our own eye. Once again, it's a matter of getting first things first. After I have shown that I am letting God's word apply to me first, *then* I can "see clearly" to help others with the speck in their eye. So as Christians, we must commit ourselves to being good examples of sincere Christian faith, listening to God's word and trying to change whenever we see that we haven't been doing right. Then, our example will lead the way as we encourage others in the things they can do better.

Second, we must commit ourselves to encouraging others to follow God's plan. It's tempting to avoid conversations about religious differences, because religion can often be a sensitive topic. We don't like tension and we often fear confrontation, so we are tempted to go along with what our culture says: everyone is okay with whatever they believe, so we shouldn't tell anyone that they might not have something right. Of course, our culture isn't God, and God shows us a different picture of how Christians should approach religious differences in Scripture.

What God shows us in Scripture is a faith that interacts with its religious neighbors and encourages them to follow God more closely. Jesus gave the mission of sharing His truth with others in Matthew 28:18-20, telling His disciples to take the gospel to all nations. With that mission in mind, Christians in the Bible were constantly talking to people about their faith and encouraging them to draw closer to God's truth. For one biblical example of many: in Acts 17:16-

17, Paul finds himself in Athens, a very divided, complex religious city. As he sees all the religion around him, he doesn't decide to leave everyone else alone. He doesn't say "oh well, everyone's already religious so I probably shouldn't say anything." Instead, Paul feels compelled to share God's truth. So he begins talking, going to the synagogue and to the marketplace, and "reasoning" with others, encouraging them to follow Jesus (verse 18). Paul loved God so much, and he loved souls so much, that he was willing to talk about religious differences and how best to follow God. We must not let culture tell us that we shouldn't discuss religion because we might offend someone. Instead of hiding from religious differences, the church must look for opportunities to discuss faith and God's truth with our religious neighbors, just like they did in the Bible.

Third, we must make sure we discuss spiritual matters with others in a spirit and tone that honors God. Too often religious conversations become religious arguments. As we discuss faith, we need to remember what Paul told Timothy about sharing God's plan:

"The Lord's bond-servant must not be quarrelsome, but be kind to all, able to teach, patient when wronged, with gentleness correcting those who are in opposition, if perhaps God may grant them repentance leading to the knowledge of the truth, and they may come to their senses and escape from the snare of the devil, having been held captive by him to do his will."
-Paul to Timothy, in 2 Timothy 2:24-26

If we are wanting to help others see and follow God's plan, we must show the attitudes Paul describes here. Not being quarrelsome. Kindness. Patient, even if we feel wronged. Gentleness. There is a right way and a wrong way to discuss religious issues. We must show love and kindness to everyone, even when we disagree. Since we are striving to genuinely love God and love people, we must learn to discuss spiritual things in a Christ-like way, without losing our tempers or being unkind.

So the church begins with some important commitments as we interacts with our religious neighbors. First, we commit ourselves to applying God's truth to ourselves before pointing out where others might be missing it. Second, we commit ourselves to be willing to discuss spiritual matters with our religious neighbors, not allowing a fear of offending people to keep us from talking about life's most important issues. Third, we commit ourselves to discussing religious matters in a genuine spirit of love and kindness. That's what Jesus commanded His followers, and that's what the church did in the Bible.

So if we are trying to simply be Christians, the way the Bible describes it, what is our relationship with the different types of religious neighbors in our lives? As we will see, encouraging others to follow God's plan includes encouraging both believers and unbelievers, people who are trying to follow Jesus as well as people who aren't. Let's look at how the Christians in Acts interacted with different types of religious neighbors.

Encouraging Those Who Don't Believe in Jesus

The first thing Christians in the Bible tried to encourage in their religious neighbors was faith in Jesus. That shouldn't surprise us, because Jesus is the beginning of our faith and message, the center from which all else proceeds (Colossians 1:18, 1 Corinthians 2:2). The Roman world was filled with idol worship, so Christians needed to tell others about the one true God and about the necessity of obeying Jesus Christ. Jesus had taught that He was the only way of salvation, as we see in places like John 14:6, where Jesus said, "I am the way, and the truth, and the life; no one comes to the Father but through Me." It is only through Jesus that we find salvation and a right relationship with God, and so the church in Acts proclaimed to their religious world just how important it is to follow Jesus:

> *"And there is salvation in no one else; for there is no other name under heaven that has been given among men by which we must be saved."*
> *-Peter and John, in Acts 4:12*

People in the religiously-divided Roman world didn't always like the message that salvation is only in Jesus – in fact the apostles faced opposition everywhere they went. And it shouldn't surprise us that some people won't like that message today either. But if Jesus was telling the truth about being the only way of salvation – and I believe He was! – and if we love people, we must try to share the way of salvation with those who don't believe in Jesus.

People sometimes say that everyone is okay spiritually as long as they are sincere in whatever their faith is. But as you read through the Book of Acts, you find Christians telling religious people that even though they were sincere, they still needed to come to Jesus, the only place where salvation and forgiveness is found. Look at a few examples of sincere religious people who still needed Jesus:

- In **Acts 2**, thousands of Jews who were "devout men" (verse 5) ask what they need to do to be right with God. Peter doesn't tell them that they are already okay because they are sincere in their religion, he tells them that Jesus is Lord, and they needed to repent and be baptized in His name (verses 36-38).

- In **Acts 8**, an Ethiopian is returning home after coming to Jerusalem to worship (verse 27-28), so he is obviously religious. As Philip approaches the chariot, the Ethiopian is even reading his Bible (verses 32-33)! Philip doesn't tell him that sincerity is enough; instead Philip preaches Jesus to him and the Ethiopian nobleman is baptized (Acts 8:35-38).
- In **Acts 10**, Cornelius is complimented as a devout man who fears God, gives generously, and prays earnestly. Those are great compliments! But his sincerity is not enough to be right with God; he still needs to hear about Jesus and be baptized, which he does (Acts 10:34-48).
- In **Acts 17**, Paul compliments the people in Athens for being "religious" (verses 22-23). But he doesn't say that being religious is enough; he tells them about the one true God, and says that they need to repent (verse 30) and follow Jesus to be right with God.
- In **Acts 23:1**, Paul says that he had always lived his life in "good conscience" before God. If you remember, Paul was killing Christians before he started following Jesus (Acts 9:1-2), because he sincerely believed it was the right thing to do. Was it okay for Paul to kill Christians since he was sincere about it? Of course not. In fact, Paul says his former life made him the "chief of sinners" (1 Timothy 1:13-16). Even though he had been sincere in his faith, he still needed to turn to Jesus and have his sins washed away in baptism to be made right with God (Acts 22:16).

As Proverbs 14:12 says it: "There is a way which seems right to a man, but its end is the way of death." The Bible is clear that just being sincere in faith doesn't make us right with God – only Jesus Christ can make us right with God. Our religious world is filled with sincere people who are following other religious faiths. God's message in the Bible is *not*, "you are sincere, so God accepts you." We must encourage them to believe in Jesus, as the Son of God and the only way of salvation.

Someone asks: Is it okay to compliment the sincerity and the good things we see in our religious neighbors of different faiths? Of course it is, just like we saw the Book of Acts compliment Cornelius and Paul compliment the people of Athens. A compliment doesn't mean we agree with everything that someone believes. But while we may indeed compliment sincerity and good qualities, we must also try to go beyond compliments: just like the Christians in the New Testament, we must encourage people to believe in and follow Jesus, the only way of salvation.

Encouraging Those Who Believe in Jesus But Haven't Been Baptized God's Way

Our religious world gets much more complex than simply those who believe in Jesus and those who don't. In American culture, the large majority of people consider themselves followers of Jesus in some way. But as you know, there is a wide spectrum of teachings and practices among those who profess Christianity. And just as the Book of Acts compliments sincere faith, we also can appreciate sincerity and good works in those who are trying to follow Jesus as best they've been taught. But here too, the Bible shows us that we must go beyond compliments, first by encouraging those who haven't been baptized God's way to take that crucial biblical step.

The first thing the apostles taught those who believed in Jesus was that they needed to be baptized into Christ. As you read through the Book of Acts, you find the importance of baptism over and over. Acts 2:37-38 sets the tone for the book, when the crowd is "pierced to the heart" by the message of Jesus. When they ask the apostles what they must do, Peter gives a clear command from God: "Repent, and each of you be baptized in the name of Jesus Christ for the forgiveness of your sins; and you will receive the gift of the Holy Spirit." He didn't say "just believe" or "just call yourself a Christian" or "say a prayer." The message of God to believers was: repent and be baptized. That message continues throughout Acts. In Acts 8, the sincere Ethiopian is not only told about Jesus, but is also taught to be baptized (Acts 8:26-39). In Acts 10, Cornelius and his household hear about Jesus, and when they believed, Peter "commanded them to be baptized in the name of Jesus Christ" (Acts 10:48). In Acts 16:25-34, the Philippian jailer is baptized in the middle of the night to become a Christian. In Acts 22, Paul tells how he became a Christian, and even though he had believed in Jesus and had been praying for three days, he was still considered a sinner in God's eyes, because God sent Ananias to tell Paul, "Now why do you delay? Get up and be baptized, and wash away your sins, calling on His name'" (Acts 22.16). We could go on. Over and over in the Book of Acts, God's plan was for believers to be baptized into Christ, at which point God gave them forgiveness and all the other spiritual blessings found in Christ.

The importance of Christian baptism in the Bible is part of the struggle in understanding our relationship with many people in today's religious world. There is no such thing as an unbaptized Christian in the New Testament, but so many people today consider themselves followers of Jesus without having been baptized into Christ the way they were in the Bible. Some of our religious neighbors have been told to pray a certain prayer to become a Christian, which you don't find in the Bible. Others have been told to be sprinkled, which you don't find in the Bible. Some have been told to be baptized, but only as a public testimony of their faith or to join a particular church, reasons for baptism that you just don't find in the Bible. Many have obeyed to the best of their knowledge, but they haven't yet done it God's way. What is God's message to those who are trying to follow Jesus, but haven't been taught biblical baptism? I believe there are at least two biblical principles we must notice and try to teach:

1) ***When Paul met people who had been baptized differently, he taught them to be baptized the right way.*** In Acts 19:1-7, Paul meets twelve men that considered themselves followers of Jesus, but in the conversation, Paul finds out that while they had been baptized, it wasn't really with the baptism of Jesus. They knew about Jesus and were trying to follow his teachings, but they hadn't been baptized to be united with Christ. Paul didn't tell them that it didn't matter, or that it was okay because they did their best. He didn't tell them that how you are baptized really isn't important. Instead, he told them to be baptized the right way, with the baptism of Jesus, and that's what they did in Acts 19:5.

   As we discuss faith with our religious neighbors, we will find many who are trying to follow Jesus but have not been baptized the way Jesus and the apostles taught it. Like Paul, we must not say "it doesn't matter," or "it's okay, you did your best." Instead, like Paul, we must encourage them to be baptized with the baptism of Jesus, both the right act (immersion in water) and the right purpose (to be united with Christ and His blessings of forgiveness and salvation).

2) ***We must try to honor the lines of Christian unity that God gives us, and baptism is one of those biblical lines.*** In Ephesians 4:1-6, Paul describes the "unity of the Spirit" (verse 3). He lists seven items that define unity with God and His people, and among the seven, Paul mentions "one baptism." Baptism is part of what defines people as Christians in God's eyes! And it doesn't say there are many baptisms to choose from, it says there is "one baptism." There is only one baptism – immersion in water into Jesus Christ – that the Bible says is necessary for sharing that "unity of the Spirit." You see the same idea in 1 Corinthians 12:13, where Paul says that while Christians have different talents and gifts, what binds us together in Christ's church is that "we were all baptized into one body."

Since the Bible says that baptism is an essential mark of Christian unity, we must honor that biblical teaching. I can be complimentary and appreciative of the good things I see in my religious neighbors who profess Christianity, but I need to be cautious about pronouncing Christian unity upon their lives if they haven't yet been baptized Christ's way. If someone *has* been baptized into Christ, I can confidently call them a brother or sister in Christ, because the Bible shows me that they have done what God commanded to be united in Christ. But if someone *has not* been baptized into Christ, I don't have an example in Scripture that describes them as part of the unity in Christ, so I must be careful not to pronounce salvation or Christian unity upon them without a word from God.

Someone may object: are you saying that everyone who hasn't been baptized the right way will be lost? I am well aware that I am not the judge, so I promise I'm not trying to say anything on my own account. I trust God to be gracious and fair and just and all-knowing in His judgment, and I will bow humbly at whatever He decides is best in eternity. I know that if God grants eternal salvation on the last day to those who did their best to become a Christian – even if they haven't been baptized the way taught in the Bible – that all of us will rejoice and be thankful, out of a love for people and their souls. But I can't make promises for God that He hasn't made. God will be the final judge of all people, including those who have never been baptized Jesus' way, but we don't get to print and hand out tickets to heaven, so we can only encourage people to be baptized God's way – where they will have God's biblical promises of salvation instead of man's promises – and leave the final judgment to Him.

It's sometimes difficult to define our relationship with the many who consider themselves Christians but haven't been baptized the Bible's way. We often have a lot in common, we often learn a lot from each other, and we often appreciate the common life goals we share. Let's be kind always, let's encourage the things we see that are good, and – just like Paul did – let's encourage those who believe in Jesus to be baptized the right way, so we can confidently say they have the salvation promises of God and biblical unity with God's people.

Encouraging Those Who Are Trying to Follow Jesus But Teach and Practice Things Differently from God's Plan

Does the Bible have a message for those who practice their faith differently from the New Testament, even if they already "go to church?" Following the example of Christians in the New Testament, we also must encourage God's way to those who are trying to follow Jesus but whose beliefs and practices are different from what is taught in the Bible. It's been a consistent theme of this book: whenever we find anyone – ourselves or others – practicing or teaching things that are different from what God wanted His church to be, we must encourage each other to go back to God's plan and do it His way. To make sure we all agree that this truly is part of what God wants us to share with our religious neighbors, look at the example of the apostle Paul.

Whenever Paul had contact with churches, Paul always encouraged them to follow God's plan more closely. Much of our New Testament is the letters of Paul to Christians and churches, and in all of those letters, Paul includes things they needed to believe more accurately or things they needed to practice more correctly. He also includes a lot of praise and thankfulness for the things they were doing well, but he doesn't ignore the ways they needed to do better in following God's plan.

Take for example the letter of 1 Corinthians. Even though the Corinthians who received Paul's letter were Christians, having all been baptized into Christ (1 Cor. 12:13), they still had many things they needed to do better. Paul had heard from some of the Corinthian Christians about divisions in the church and how some were claiming human names in their faith (1 Cor. 1:10-13); he had heard how the church was allowing some to openly live in sin without calling them to repent (1 Cor. 5); how fellow Christians were taking each other to court (1 Cor. 6); and how their worship services were so chaotic and self-centered that they dishonored God (1 Cor. 11:17-34 and 1 Cor. chapter 14). He had heard about things they didn't teach like they should, such as proper sexual morality (1 Cor. 6:12-7:40) and the reality of resurrection on the last day (1 Cor. 15).

What we need to notice is how Paul handled it when he heard about these things in the Corinthian church. He did not say: "Oh well, at least they're going to church, I won't say anything to them." Paul doesn't ignore the ways they were missing God's plan. Instead, Paul wrote the letter we call 1 Corinthians, and he also planned to come talk to them face to face, encouraging them to follow all of God's plan to the best of their ability. So we see a great example for addressing religious differences in 1 Corinthians: Paul praises them for the good things they were doing and lets them know that he loves them (1 Cor. 1:1-9, for example), but he also he discusses the things they needed to change to better obey God's plan.

As we discuss spiritual matters with our religious neighbors, we again must follow the example of Paul. Let's not just ignore our religious differences when we see they don't match up with God's plan. Let's not think, "oh well, they're trying, so surely God doesn't care about the ways they could be more faithful." Instead, let's love God's plan for the church enough – and love people enough – to encourage them to follow God's plan more closely.

Someone may object: shouldn't we just focus on what we have in common with those trying to follow Jesus and not focus on our differences? We should certainly praise and compliment what is good in God's eyes wherever we see it, just like Paul did. And we certainly have more important things to "focus" on than just the differences of our religious neighbors – but that doesn't mean we ignore those differences, either. The bottom line, to me: if Paul believed it was important to point the Corinthian church (and many other churches) toward following God's plan more closely in the ways they had been missing it, we must do the same.

With all the different teachings and practices in our religious world, we probably need to discuss our differences more than we do – in the spirit and kindness of Christ – to help each other see God's way as best we can. After all, Jesus was very clear that it's possible to call yourself a Christian and do lots of "Christian things" and still not be right with God (Matthew 7:21-27). So we must try to encourage everyone to follow God's truth, even those who already consider themselves Christians. God will be the final judge of hearts and motives and shortcomings, in a way that none of us can, so we must always acknowledge God's role as the eternal judge. But for those of us who are not the final judge: in our complex religious world, with so many churches doing so many different things, we must lean on Scripture and encourage others to follow it in every way. We may be surprised to see how many honest-hearted people there are, people who sincerely want to follow God's way above all else.

The Church of Christ

Trying to simply be Christians and follow God's plan in a divided religious world is not easy. And trying to determine our relationship with religious neighbors who don't share those same commitments is one of the more difficult questions we wrestle with. I hope that looking at how the New Testament church engaged people in different religious situations helps us understand God's message to each of those groups, messages that we must continue to share today.

In the New Testament, Christians loved God enough to apply His truth to themselves first, and they loved people enough to discuss God's truth with others in a spirit of genuine love. When they met people who didn't believe in Jesus, Christians encouraged them to believe in and follow God's only Son, the only way to salvation. When they talked with people who did believe in Jesus, Christians encouraged them to be baptized into Christ. If those who believed had not been baptized God's way, the apostles encouraged them to do it right, to put their hope of salvation on the promises of God rather than the promises of men. When they talked with people who were already "going to church" and trying to follow Jesus, the apostles still encouraged them to follow God's plan more closely in every way, in their teaching and practice, in their lives and in their churches. In every situation, God's people were constantly pointing others towards God's plan. In our own divided religious world, we must try to do the same: starting with ourselves, let's point all people, including our many religious neighbors, toward the plan of God.

What's Next...

We've covered a lot of ground in this book! We have seen that the church really is important to God, and that what the church teaches and practices really is important to God. We have studied some ways we believe our religious world needs to get back to God's biblical plan for His church. We have studied the big picture of what the church is supposed to be doing: operating upward, inward, and outward. And we have studied some difficult questions that come up as we try to pursue New Testament Christianity in a divided religious world, questions that help us think deeper about our goals and our message.

Before we end this study, let's take a final chapter and see a good picture of how this all fits together. We'll do that by looking at a church in the Bible that shows us what God wanted His church to be. I'm sure they weren't perfect, because their church was filled with people like all churches are, but they modeled the goals and commitments God wanted His church to uphold. Perhaps we can learn something from them as we try to make the church all that God wants it to be in our own day...

Discussion Questions

1) In Matthew 7:1-5, is Jesus saying that we shouldn't tell others what they need to change to help them be right with God? What is He saying?
2) If someone were to approach you about something they thought you needed to change spiritually, what attitude would you want them to have? What kinds of attitudes lead to arguments about religious differences?

3) Is it okay to compliment good things we see in people of different religious backgrounds? What examples in the Bible show us it's okay to compliment good things in people who still have a lot they need to change? Does a compliment mean you agree with everything someone believes or does?

4) Is sincerity enough to be right with God? What biblical examples or verses help us answer that question?

5) Is it possible for someone who calls themselves a Christian and does "Christian things" not to be right with God? Read Matthew 7:21-23 for help. Then read Matthew 7:24-27. What is Jesus teaching?

6) What does Acts 19:1-7 tell us about how seriously God wants us to take "being baptized the right way?" From that example, what do you think Paul would tell someone today who believed in Jesus but had not been baptized the "right way?"

7) What does Ephesians 4:1-6 tell us about what it means to be a Christian? What are the 7 defining characteristics mentioned in that passage that make up the "unity of the Spirit?" Does that list help us understand where God draws His lines of Christian unity?

8) When Christians and churches were doing things differently from God's plan, did the apostles ignore their shortcomings, or did they encourage them to change? What examples can you think of?

9) What do you think about the idea that we should focus on what we have in common with others who are trying to follow Jesus instead of talking about differences? Do you agree, disagree, or a little of both?

How does Paul's example help us answer that question?

10) Read John 12:48. Who is the final judge in eternity? Is it possible to share God's truth with others without acting like we are the judge?

11) This chapter repeatedly used the word "encourage" to describe how we show others the ways they can better follow God's plan. Do you like that description for faith conversations? Can you think of a better term to describe it? Can you think of one that would be worse?

Personal Reflection

1) Do I ever have religious conversations with others? How could I do that more in the future? What good things might come from it?
2) Do I live the type of life that allows people to see that I am sincerely (though imperfectly) trying to follow Christ? If not, what do I need to do better?
3) Do you know people whose faith is so sincere that you would gladly listen if they approached you in love about a spiritual matter they believed you needed to change or do better? Why would you listen to them? Are there some people you know that you would not listen to? Why not?
4) Have I been baptized into Christ? If not, why not? Was my baptism different than the baptism we find in the New Testament? What might Paul tell me if my baptism was different from biblical baptism?

Final Chapter:
Putting It All Together

CHAPTER 13

Becoming The Church God Wants Us To Be

"...And for an entire year they met with the church and taught considerable numbers; and the disciples were first called Christians in Antioch."
-Acts 11:26

Starters

- What makes a successful church in God's eyes?
- Do you think our world defines church success differently than God does? If so, how?
- Glance through Revelation chapters 2 and 3 at Christ's letters to the seven churches. Notice what Jesus approves of, and notice what He disapproves of. Does that help us see what God thinks is important in a church?

A Successful Church, From God's Perspective

What makes a successful church? In a culture that (sadly) often measures churches according to business or entertainment standards, that can be a difficult question. Is church success dependent on how big the church is? How fast its numbers are growing? How popular it is in the community? How exciting its preacher or worship is? How well it keeps up with the latest trends? Just listing those questions should remind us that they really aren't the most important questions, even though people sometimes act like they are. Surely God desires His church to pursue deeper things than those surface-level standards, which often feel like they are based in human popularity more than anything else.

If we want to properly understand church success, we need to know Revelation chapters 2 and 3, where we get a glimpse of how Jesus feels about what's important in the church. (We took a brief look at this passage back in Chapter 3.) In those chapters, Jesus has the apostle John write to seven churches in the Roman province of Asia, and we find Jesus sharing what He is proud of and what disappoints Him. Among other things, it shows us that God will reject churches that stop pursuing His goals in favor of their own goals. So it is a valuable section of Scripture for making sure our churches are truly honoring Christ. If you were just to read through those chapters, making a list of what Jesus approved and disapproved of, I think it would be worth your time. I'll go ahead and tell you what you don't find in those chapters: Jesus says nothing about how many people were in the church. He says nothing about how fast they were growing or shrinking. He doesn't care whether they were keeping up with the trends, or whether they had a great reputation in the community, or whether their preacher was "dynamic." Instead, you find Jesus evaluating those churches based on deeper things. Jesus measures those churches based on whether they truly had a love for Him, whether they were faithfully teaching God's truth, whether they were persevering in faith through persecution and difficult times, whether they were alive in their faith, whether they were properly addressing sin or false teaching, and whether they were truly giving effort to living out God's plan.

Isn't it interesting how God's view of a church can be so different from man's view? The only time Jesus mentions reputation in those chapters is to tell the church in Sardis that even though they had a great reputation as a church, Jesus knew that they were actually spiritually dead (Rev. 3:1). Earthly popularity and reputation isn't the same as being pleasing to God. The only time Jesus mentions wealth is to tell the church at Laodicea that even though they thought they were wealthy, they were actually poor, spiritually speaking (Rev. 3:17). Earthly wealth is not the same as spiritual wealth. The world values worldly things, even in churches. Jesus cares about faithfulness to Him and His plan.

Those chapters also make me wonder how often today we might see growing or trendy churches that people think are wonderful, not knowing that God might not be pleased with those churches, if they have sacrificed faithfulness to Him in order to please more people. I wonder if the church God is most pleased with could be one that doesn't meet any of the worldly standards for a popular church. It might be a small church. It might be in a small town. They might not be interested in any of the latest worship or outreach trends. But who knows, even if people aren't impressed, God may be most pleased with that church, because they are faithfully following Him and His plan with their whole heart. Let me be clear: growing churches aren't necessarily bad and small churches aren't necessarily good, and I certainly don't know what church God is most pleased with. But I do know that God sees things differently than man sees them (1 Samuel 16:7, Isaiah 55:8-9), and sometimes our standards for a great church are not God's standards for a great church.

So if we truly want to make our churches pleasing to God (and I hope we do!), we want to make sure we value the things that God values. We don't want to get too caught up trying to chase whatever people think makes a church great or exciting. And sometimes simply reminding ourselves that our highest goal in the church is to honor and please God – and not just to please people – is an important first step.

Making a Difference in the World

When people hear that the church should focus on pleasing God over pleasing people, they sometimes respond: but shouldn't the church be trying to make an impact in the world? And the answer, of course, is absolutely we should! I think we will all agree, impacting the world is indeed a big reason Christ established the church. The church is God's plan for taking the message of Jesus and changing the world with it. Remember, Jesus' followers are the ones who are salt and light in the world, bringing glory to God as people see God's goodness in us (Matthew 5:13-16). The church is the place where God's gospel – the power of God to salvation (Romans 1:16) – is lived out and shared with others. Look at what Paul says about the church as the channel that makes God's wisdom known:

"so that the manifold wisdom of God might now be made known <u>through the church</u> to the rulers and the authorities in the heavenly places."
-Ephesians 3:10

The church is the place where God's truth – the most important message of life – is spread throughout the world! And in the very next verse, Paul makes it clear that God's plan for the church to play that all-important role was God's plan from all eternity:

"This was in accordance with <u>the eternal purpose</u> which He carried out in Christ Jesus our Lord."
-Ephesians 3:11

God has always had high hopes for His church: hopes that His church would impact the world as salt and light, making God's wisdom known to all men.

So yes, the church should absolutely be trying to make an impact on the world. And I'm convinced that the best way for the church to make a real spiritual impact on the world is by focusing on pleasing God and following His plan. The best way is *not* to try to improve on God's plan by changing teachings people don't like, attempting to be more popular with the surrounding culture. The best way is *not* to think we can improve on biblical worship practices or church organization practices or make other man-made changes, somehow believing our ways will be better for spiritual growth than the ways God gave us in Scripture.

There are at least two reasons why I believe going back to God's plan for His church is the best way to impact the world. *First,* I trust that the eternal God knows the best plan for His church, a plan that will produce genuine spiritual impact. If God wanted the church to impact the world, and that was His plan from all eternity, don't you think God would've set up the church with the right teachings and practices to truly bring about spiritual growth? If there was a way to improve the spiritual impact of the church, God would've given it to His people. He knew the best way for the church to honor Him and reach out to the world, and that's how He set it up. If we think we can improve on God's plan for His church, we might need to rethink what we really believe about God's eternal wisdom. *Second*, the Bible teaches that genuine spiritual impact comes from God Himself. In 1 Corinthians chapter 3, Paul says that when the people of Corinth became Christians, it wasn't really because of Paul or Apollos, who were merely servants to whom God gave the opportunity to teach. Then look at what he says in verses 6-7:

> *"I planted, Apollos watered, but God was causing the growth. So then neither the one who plants nor the one who waters is anything, but God who causes the growth."*

I think you will find that principle throughout the Bible, including the church's amazing growth in the Book of Acts: God is the one who produces the growth of His word and His kingdom. If we want to impact the world, we need God's blessing! And the way to make sure we have the blessing of God is to trust and follow His plan.

So I believe faithfulness to God's plan is the best way to impact the world, because it trusts both God's wisdom and God's blessing. The church shouldn't have to choose between being faithful to God or being missional for God. If we want to be missional as a church – not just people-pleasing, but truly missional – then we need to make faithfulness to God's plan our first concern. That's what the church did in the Bible, and God used their faith to make a great impact on their world. In fact, that's how we will bring this study toward a close: let's look in the Bible to see how passion for God and His plan led one church to make a great spiritual impact, an example I hope will help us think about how God can do the same thing through us today.

A Church That Impacted the World

The Book of Acts tells us about the spread of the gospel and the church in the first generation after Jesus' death, resurrection, and ascension. The church began in Jerusalem in Acts chapter 2, and that first church had a big impact on the city of Jerusalem (see Acts 2:42-47, 5:28). It wasn't a perfect church, of course – they had disagreements and they had to deal with hypocrites, like many churches do – but as a whole, they faithfully pursued God's plan and made a difference in changing lives for Christ.

After the Jewish leaders began persecuting the Jerusalem church harshly in Acts chapters 7-8, Christians from Jerusalem scattered all over the Roman empire. And one of the places they came to was a city called Antioch, where there would grow one of the great churches we find in the Bible. It was a church that was fully committed to God's plan, including a desire to make a difference in the world for God. Look at Acts 11:19-26:

> *(19) So then those who were scattered because of the persecution that occurred in connection with Stephen made their way to Phoenicia and Cyprus and Antioch, speaking the word to no one except to Jews alone.*
> *(20) But there were some of them, men of Cyprus and Cyrene, who came to Antioch and began speaking to the Greeks also, preaching the Lord Jesus.*
> *(21) And the hand of the Lord was with them, and a large*

number who believed turned to the Lord.
(22) The news about them reached the ears of the church at Jerusalem, and they sent Barnabas off to Antioch.
(23) Then when he arrived and witnessed the grace of God, he rejoiced and began to encourage them all with resolute heart to remain true to the Lord;
(24) for he was a good man, and full of the Holy Spirit and of faith. And considerable numbers were brought to the Lord.
(25) And he left for Tarsus to look for Saul;
(26) and when he had found him, he brought him to Antioch. And for an entire year they met with the church and taught considerable numbers; and the disciples were first called Christians in Antioch.

What an amazing passage about an amazing church! The Antioch church quickly began making an impact in their community, as it says a "large number" turned to the Lord (v. 21), and "considerable numbers" (v. 24,26) were taught and brought to the Lord. God is not against large numbers in a church – in fact, God wants everyone to be saved! Our point earlier was that numbers alone are not the measure of church success in God's eyes. Here, we see that God blessed the faithfulness of the Antioch church with great growth in the number of people coming to Christ. God's blessing on their work was soon heard back in Jerusalem (v. 22), and when Barnabas came and saw it firsthand, he couldn't help but "rejoice" at what God was doing in Antioch (v. 23).

Antioch not only grew as a local church, encouraging many to give their lives to Christ, but they also helped Christ's church throughout the Roman world. The Antioch church sent relief to the poor Christians in Jerusalem when they heard that a famine was coming (Acts 11:27-30). And it was the Antioch church that sent Paul and Barnabas off (through the command of God) on their missionary journeys to plant churches all over the Roman empire, starting in Acts 13:1-3. What's more, Antioch was the first place that disciples were called "Christians" (Acts 11:26), as their community noticed their commitment to following Jesus Christ. What can we learn from the Antioch church about making an impact for God?

Antioch: Qualities Worth Imitating

That passage in Acts 11 says that the Antioch church had the "hand of the Lord with them" (Acts 11:21) and the "grace of God" (Acts 11:23), which led to them making such a difference for Christ. What did the Antioch church do so well that led to God's blessing in impacting their world?

1. **They practiced Christian community**. This was a church made up of both Jews and Gentiles (verses 19-20), bringing different backgrounds together in a way that I'm sure wasn't always easy. In Acts 13:1, we see the list of teachers at Antioch, a diverse group that most scholars agree probably consisted of men from various racial and economic backgrounds – different races, different skin colors, and different levels of wealth and education, all serving together toward the common goal of living for Jesus Christ.

   Don't you suppose that strong sense of community in the Antioch church made a difference in their impact? Jesus had told the apostles that the world would be able to recognize them as His followers by the love they had for one another (John 13:34-35). I'm sure it got the attention of the people in Antioch to see such a diverse group working together toward a common life goal. What could have been so important, they must have asked, to bring this group of people together in such a strong bond?

Christ's church today is a global community of different races, languages, ages, skin colors, and economic backgrounds, and while not every local church has such diversity in their individual church family, each congregation should honor the church's global diversity, and it must show love toward everyone they come in contact with, no matter their background. When the church shows unity and love for each other and for people of all ages, races, and backgrounds, we are showing the love of Christ, and showing people that Christianity is bigger than the divisive lines that are often drawn by men.

2. **They practiced Christian commitment**. In Acts 11:19-20, we saw that the Antioch church was established by Christians who were so committed to Christ that they would not allow even physical persecution to stop them from teaching and living Jesus Christ. They left the persecution in Jerusalem and came to Antioch, and immediately began preaching Jesus there too. This was a committed church, a commitment that included meeting together often (v. 26), and no doubt their commitment also got the city's attention. In fact, when Barnabas came to encourage them, he urged them to "remain true to the Lord" (v. 23). Barnabas could see that their commitment to the Lord was the key to all the good things God was doing through them.

The church today also must live out a commitment to the Lord that is worth noticing. Didn't Jesus say that His followers were supposed to deny themselves and take up their cross and follow Him (Matthew 16:24)? Too often, churches display a half-hearted commitment to God, allowing a love for the world to hold back their personal willingness to sacrifice for Christ. We are tempted to sacrifice more for much less-worthy causes, like jobs, sports, schools, and politics, until our faith looks like a much lower priority than it should be. If we want to make an impact for Christ, our commitment to Christ above all else should be one of the first things people notice about us.

3. **They practiced Christian communication**. Notice that the Antioch church had a message! What was it? Verse 20 says they were "preaching the Lord Jesus." When people heard what they were teaching, they turned "to the Lord" (v. 21,24,26), not to a trendy philosophy or a denominational group, but to Christ Himself. If we could've heard their message, we would've heard them preaching and talking about Jesus. As the Bible shows, preaching Jesus leads people to be baptized into Jesus (Acts 8:35-38) and to follow all of His commandments (Matthew 28:18-20). The Antioch church knew they had the message of salvation through Christ, the most important message in all the world, and they didn't hide it – they shared it in teaching and conversation all over the city. Then, when they sent Paul and Barnabas out for their missionary journeys, they helped send that message of Jesus all over the Roman world.

   The church today also must practice Christian communication, by teaching Jesus and encouraging others to come to Him. Remember, the church has the job of sharing God's wisdom with all creation (Eph. 3:10, 1 Tim. 3:15), so the church has a God-given, all-important message. We must never allow that message to be watered down by people-pleasing or religious trends or politics or anything else. And notice that while living as a good example in the world is crucial, a good example is not all that the church is supposed to be doing. We must look to *communicate*, to actually speak and share the message of Christ through conversations and invitations, teaching publicly and privately. We don't always know how best to share the gospel with others in a way that they will listen, but we must do our best to teach and preach Jesus, and trust that God will open doors and give the increase.

4. **They practiced Christian compassion.** In Acts 11:27-30, God spoke through a prophet named Agabus (prophecy was a gift of the Holy Spirit in the days of the apostles). Agabus told the church at Antioch that there would soon be a famine all over the world (v. 28), and notice what the church did in verses 29-30: they contributed together as much as they could, and sent a relief fund to the church around Jerusalem, which was known to have many who were poor. Think about that. Instead of saying "we'd better start saving up for ourselves to make it through the famine," which would have been a perfectly understandable response, their first thought was, "we need to help our brothers and sisters who are poor." Once again, the Antioch church is following the example of Jesus, who put others ahead of Himself throughout His ministry, healing and helping others in need. As Paul wrote years later to some of those churches he established on his first missionary journey: "So then, while we have opportunity, let us do good to all people, and especially to those who are of the household of faith" (Galatians 6:10). I can't help but think part of the Antioch church's success in bringing

people to Christ was that people could see their Christ-like compassion for other people.

The church today also must practice Christian compassion. We live in a selfish world, and so Christian compassion not only honors God, but it stands out as different and better than what people are used to seeing. We must look around our communities and our world for ways to show God's love to those who are hurting, following the example of Jesus Himself, and also of churches like Antioch. Christian compassion opens doors for the gospel, both in the hearts of those who are helped and in the hearts of those who notice the goodness of such Christ-like acts.

5. **They were simply being Christians**. Isn't it interesting that of all places, it was the church right there in Antioch where the disciples were first called "Christians" (Acts 11:26). All the things they were doing – their community, their commitment, their communication, and their compassion – were following the example and teaching of Jesus Christ, and people couldn't help but notice the connection. And notice that "Christian" was the only name they took. They didn't call themselves Paul-Christians or Peter-Christians or any of the denominational and divisive add-on names people put on their faith today. They were simply Christians, followers of Jesus Christ.

   The church today should also be known as simply "Christians." All that we do should reflect the example and teaching of Jesus Christ, and people should be able to notice the connection, not just because we go meet in a church building, but because we live and teach something special, something that comes from Jesus

> Himself. And like the disciples in the Bible, we must only take the name of Jesus. God doesn't want us to take human names or denominational names, He wants us to simply be Christians. When we are simply Christians – in name, in teaching, in practice – we are following in the line of great churches like Antioch, churches who were committed to following the plan God gave His church. And like Antioch, we trust that being Christians according to God's plan will result in God giving the increase to our efforts, helping us make an impact for Christ on our families, our communities, and our world.

So what did the Antioch church do in order to make such an impact on souls, both in their community and around the world? They simply lived faithful, committed Christian lives according to the plan of God. If we think we need to somehow improve God's plan for His church in order to make a difference for God, we are missing a key message of the New Testament: the way to make an impact for God is by trusting His way and His blessing. All the things men have changed in God's plan for His church through the years? They are not improvements, and they won't bring the genuine spiritual impact that God's plan will. God will lead the way, if only we will be faithful enough to trust Him. The message of Jesus is so powerful that whenever it is lived out in all its goodness and faithfulness, it cannot help but make an impact wherever it goes. It won't always produce growth in numbers, because people must make their own faith decisions, but it will always draw people to make deeper decisions about God, because "a city set on a hill cannot be hidden" (Matthew 5:14). Let's do things God's way, trusting God's wisdom and God's blessing, and we will see God use us to make an impact for Him, just as He has used faithful churches in the past like the one in Antioch.

The Church of Christ

I hope this book has helped us see how important the church is to God, and how important it is for the church to follow God's plan. God's plan from all eternity was for Jesus to establish His church, and the church is still His plan! Here are a few final thoughts to bring it all together:

If you are not part of churches of Christ, those of us who are trying to simply be Christians: I hope this study has encouraged you to think about why it's so important to follow God's plan for His church. We would love for you to join us in showing the world it's possible to simply be a Christian and just follow the Bible, even in a divided religious world. We are not perfect, we fall short like everyone else, but we believe we are pursuing the right goals, the goals God gave His church. While there is no such thing as a perfect church, there is a difference between churches who continually pursue the plan of God and churches that have stopped pursuing God's goals because they are too caught up in human goals. We hope you will join us in seeing the goodness and the world-changing potential of biblical Christianity.

If you are already part of churches of Christ, those of us trying to simply be part of the one church Christ established: let's re-commit ourselves to that beautiful goal of simply being Christians. Our divided religious world discourages us, and sadly most people have accepted the type of division that God never wanted. Let's show our world that God has a better way, if only we are willing to drop our denominational names and practices and our people-pleasing tendencies, and go back to restoring God's plan for His church. I believe many of our honest-hearted religious neighbors would be happy to see that New Testament Christianity is really possible, and they need to see and hear it in us, in a spirit that shows the love of God.

The church is still God's plan and God's instrument for changing the world! Let's live out a commitment to making Christ's church everything He wanted it to be. Let's drop all the ways we have messed up God's plan, and let's get back to operating upwards, inwards, and outwards, just like they did in the New Testament. When we do that, I trust we will have God's blessing upon us, and I have no doubt that we will see God work through us in great ways.

What's Next...

What's next is for you and I to try to make the church everything God wanted it to be, to the best of our ability! In many ways this book just gives some starting points, but starting points are important! There are many questions left to be answered, about what the Bible teaches on a variety of issues. But if we can commit ourselves to the importance of the church, to simply being undenominational Christians, to practicing things in the church as we see in Scripture, and being willing to change anything that we find different from God's plan, then we are starting down a great path, a path that best leads us toward God's plan for His people. And I believe that when we trust God enough to do things His way, we will move closer to the unity and the impact that He wants His church to have. Let's show everyone that it's possible to be the undenominational, biblical church of Christ in today's world...

Discussion Questions

1) Does God expect His church to make an impact in the world? What passages of Scripture teach us that?

2) Do you think some people in our religious world act as if we can improve on God's biblical plan for His church?
3) Do you think God's plan for the church can be improved by men? Why or why not?
4) Do you believe that God gives the increase for His church? How do you think He does that?
5) Read Acts 2:42-47 about the church in Jerusalem. Do you see the church operating upward, inward, and outward in that passage?
6) As you read Acts 11:19-30 and Acts 13:1-3, what do you appreciate about the church in Antioch? What impact did they make on their world?
7) Of the things this chapter says Antioch did well – community, commitment, communication, compassion – which one do you think is easiest? Which do you think is most difficult?
8) What does it mean for a church to be both faithful and missional? Should we have to choose one or the other?
9) What are some things that you take away from this book, things you think you will remember?
10) Do you think people would appreciate the message of simply being undenominational Christians if they understood it correctly? How can we best share it?

Personal Reflection

1) Am I part of a church that pursues undenominational, biblical Christianity? If not, why not?
2) Of the things the church at Antioch did well – community, commitment, communication, and compassion – am

I helping God's church build any of them? Which ones can I help with that I haven't been helping with?

3) How can I share the message of simply being Christians with others? Do I believe it's the right message?